Paul A. Samuelson:

On Being an Economist

Paul A. Samuelson:
On Being an Economist

Michael Szenberg,
Aron A. Gottesman,
and Lall Ramrattan

With Foreword by Joseph E. Stiglitz

Jorge Pinto Books, Inc.
New York

Paul A. Samuelson: On Being an Economist

Paul A. Samuelson: On Being an Economist is the first book in the *Working
Biographies* series.

Published by Jorge Pinto Books Inc., website: www.pintobooks.com
Book production supervised by Mimi Pagsibigan.
Cover design © 2005 by Nigel Holmes, website: www.nigelholmes.com
Book design by Charles King, website: www.ckmm.com

Trade Paperback ISBN 0-9742615-3-X
E-book ISBN 0-9742615-4-8

First Printing: May 2005.
Second Printing: October 2005.

Contents

B"H

Dedicated to the memory of my sister, Esther;
to my children Naomi and Avi and
their spouses Marc and Tova;
to my grandchildren
Elki, Batya, Chanoch, Devorah, Ephraim, Ayala, and Jacob;
to my wife, Miriam, for her enthusiastic devotion
to the grandchildren
–M.S.

To my wife, Ronit;
and to my children
Libby Leah, Yakov Tzvi,
Raphael Yehuda, and Tzipora Genendel
–A.A.G.

To my wife, Noreena;
to my children
Devi and her husband Arjun, Shanti, Hari, and Rani;
and to my grandchildren
Soham and Lakshmi
–L.R.

B"H

I do not know what I may appear to the world, but to myself I seem to have been only like a boy playing on the seashore, and diverting myself in now and then finding a prettier shell or a smoother pebble than ordinary whilst the great ocean of truth lay all undiscovered about me.

Isaac Newton

I am a social scientist before I am an economist and a scientist before I am a social scientist— and, I hope, a human being before either of the others.

Herbert Simon

Men with vision walk in the Middle.

Tosefta: Babba Kama

Foreword by Joseph E. Stiglitz

THIS BOOK captures much of the spirit of Paul A. Samuelson. Those who know Samuelson, one of the great economists of the twentieth century, only through his writings may have already sensed his wit, his intellect, his brilliance. This book brings these into focus, through details of his personal history and a wealth of anecdotes from colleagues and students.

I became a student of Paul in the fall of 1963, as part of the entering class at MIT. But my debt of gratitude—beyond the usual debt that everyone in the profession owes him for having crystallized so many central ideas—predates that. He was responsible for my being at MIT. As a junior, late in the spring of 1963, I decided that I wanted to switch from majoring in physics to economics. My advisor, Ralph Beals, called Paul and urged him to accept me—late as it was, and with no college degree—into the Ph.D. program.

I loved my MIT courses—but especially I loved my classes with Samuelson. The first half hour (sometimes the first hour, occasionally, the first hour and a half) was often spent on what appeared to be some digression, some comment on the history of the field. Oblique references might or might not be picked up and developed further later. Then, in the last few minutes of the class, he would turn to the mimeographed notes that he had prepared and bring it all together. He always provided fresh insights beyond anything one could get from any text. I had come to MIT to see great minds in action, and Samuelson more than satisfied what I had hoped to get.

The following summer, Paul asked me to be his research assistant, to help edit and organize what were to be the first two volumes of his collected papers. What a way to study for one's comprehensive exams! I figured that if I understood Samuelson's papers, I understood modern economics. Samuelson had achieved a breadth of contributions that was truly enviable—without sacrificing depth in any way. He had shown that, in matters of intellect, there did not have to be trade-offs. Quite the contrary—it was only in seeing all of the parts that one could understand the whole. If one really wanted to understand our economic system, one could not be just a macroeconomist or a microeconomist; one could not ignore finance, but one could not just be a finance economist. One had to understand growth and economic dynamics; but one also had to understand the principles of static resource allocation. Indeed, from his earliest work, *The Foundations of Economic Analysis*, he looked for an underlying unity.

There is another sense in which Samuelson might have been seen to repeal the usual laws of economics. Samuelson had not only an absolute advantage, but a comparative advantage, in both exposition and research. His textbook, *Economics*, was a landmark. Others might have done almost as good a job in explaining the principles of economics. They might have gotten things a little wrong, missed some of the subtleties, but these were distinctions that would have been lost on most undergraduates anyway. But who would have discovered the factor-price equalization theorem? Who else would have developed the theory of revealed preference or the overlapping generations model? Who could have articulated the pure theory of public goods? Would Samuelson have given us even more nuggets, enough to keep another generation of economists engaged in filling out the details, if he had devoted himself 100% to his research? The very idea is daunting, and one can only speculate—but I think in many ways the two activities were complementary. It was because he understood the ideas so clearly that he could articulate them so well; and, perhaps, as he strove to refine the articulation, he generated ideas that his always-engaged mind would eventually develop into precise mathematical models.

I suppose our paths were destined to cross. We were both from the same steel-making town of Gary, Indiana, though my family remained decades after his family had left. Like Paul, my mother (born a year earlier) received her undergraduate degree from the University of Chicago—mostly because, in the Great Depression, one had no choice but to go to the local college. I'm sure that the poverty, inequality, unemployment, and discrimination that one could not miss growing up in Gary must have had some of the same effect on Samuelson that it had on me. These were the central problems of our society—how could one not want to do something about them? And how could one really believe that markets, by themselves, were solving these problems—or would ever provide a full resolution?

To understand Samuelson, though, one has to understand that his strong social ethic is mixed with a deep intellectual commitment, a love of mathematics and of ideas. The ideas carried him along, where they might. Sometimes, as in the development of the pure theory of public goods, they provided fundamental insights into the appropriate role of government; or, as in the pure consumption loans model, into the dynamics of growth and the role of social security. He understood the role of markets, but he also understood their limitations. He understood the uses of mathematics, and he, more than perhaps anyone else, developed the MIT style of using "small" models to understand the workings of the economy. General theories—in which one could say little more than that an equilibrium exists—were of limited value. He wanted to say more, and he showed the world how one could say so much more, if only one crafted one's model carefully and thoughtfully.

For those of Samuelson's generation, the Great Depression was the defining event, Keynesian economics the revolution in ideas. Classical economics could not explain the Depression, and with the abandonment of classical economics, how was one to retain faith in market economics? Some of the earlier generation buried their heads in the sand and denied, or at least did everything they could to minimize the extent of, the problem. In the heady days of growth theory at MIT, we were once lectured on putty-clay growth models—where capital was malleable before it was put into concrete form, but not after—and warned of a similar problem in human capital. We would be molded for life by what we learned in these three or four years; a few of the more lucky might be able to break out of the mold, but for the rest of us our present was our future. Though put forward as mere description of reality, the warning itself was part of our MIT education, what we would carry forward as part of our intellectual capital. Samuelson, in spite of his Chicago training, was not fully vested in the

classical model and became one of those in the forefront
of the Keynesian revolution. And yet, through his classical
synthesis, he tried to preserve as much of classical economics as possible.

But still, even setting aside Keynesian unemployment
problems, Samuelson never fully believed, I think, in the
perfection of the markets. At least that was the conclusion
I came to as a result of the diatribes we heard against the
extremism of Chicago economics, and its blind faith in
markets. It was this as much as anything else that set me
on the road to more deeply questioning the assumptions
underlying the neoclassical model, assumptions such as
those associated with perfect and symmetric information
and complete markets. I was more convinced by the criti-
cisms of "Chicago" economics than by the simple models
of perfect competition and perfect markets, in which
Chicago economics might have actually made some sense.
Models help guide our thinking, but we should never let
the analysis of simple models replace our thinking, or let
us lose touch with reality—including the realities that
brought us to economics in the first place.

I was fortunate to be a student of Paul Samuelson—not
just the kind of student that the entire economics profession has been for more than sixty years, learning from his
voluminous written works, but a "first hand student." As
a student, there is, I think, no greater tribute that I could
give than this: He was a role model, one which ever since
I have sought to emulate.

Preface

JEWISH FOLKLORE tells of a poor man requesting a favor
from the banker Baron Rothschild: to allow him to accom-
pany Rothschild as he paced through the stock exchange.
To the financier's query about how this would improve the
poor man's position, the latter replied, "Well, just being
seen in your company will establish my financial standing." Paul A. Samuelson is the intellectual Rothschild for
many thousands of students who moved through the halls
of economics at his side.[1]

When Jorge Pinto, the CEO of Pinto Books, approached
us to write a biography of an economist, we immediately
suggested Paul A. Samuelson.[2] Pinto Books has launched
a series of beautifully designed books, each profiling one
leader in a number of disciplines such as physics, sociology, and medicine. The biographies focus on the discipline
through the lens of one outstanding scholar.

The choice of Paul A. Samuelson was easy. He dazzles us
with an overwhelming display of learning, insight, energy,
aplomb, modesty, profundity, and an amazing inventive-
ness. He single-handedly revitalized and transformed the
discipline of economics. Furthermore, he represents the
best that the economics discipline has given us. Through
his work, friendship, and fellowship he has touched, and
changed unalterably, many lives. Paul A. Samuelson, or
PAS as he refers to himself, the master of prose and humor,
has a magical ability to connect with an audience, and is
admired by the economic community as a whole. It is rare,

indeed, to find conversation, correspondence, and scholarship so well blended in one person.

Perry Mehrling of Columbia University relates a characteristic story of Samuelson: "[He] mentioned that he had heard about a piece I had written on Irving Fisher. I have no idea how he heard about it, but I offered to send him a copy and within a few days I got back a letter, dated 27 May 2003. He had read the paper and wanted to set down his own interpretation, but then he closes the letter with a remarkable line that I treasure: 'Do disregard my heresies and follow your own star.' "[3]

Samuelson's embrace of younger scholars leads to the nurturing and development of many great minds. It is revealing to contrast Samuelson's behavior with someone of novelist Marcel Proust's stature. Whenever Proust, whose writings critics compare to Homer, Dante, and Shakespeare, was asked to evaluate a manuscript, he always enclosed the following letter: "Divine work. It is a work of genius. I would not change a word. I take my hat off for you. All the best, Marcel Proust."[4] He wrote the same laudatory note to all potential writers who contacted him. When confronted about what he was doing, Proust said that he did not have time to read the submitted material because it interfered with his writing. By telling young authors that their work was that of a genius, he made sure that they would not return their revised papers to him with changes. Proust's behavior, though amusing and seemingly innocent, illustrates the gross impediments the turn of the century classical author was willing to place before fledgling writers, thereby violating an important moral principle: "Before the blind do not put a stumbling block." Samuelson would find such a deceitful act abhorrent.

There is a widely exaggerated and stereotyped notion shared by many that superior scientists can neither lead a balanced life nor be paragons of virtue. Consider the words of William Butler Yeats, the poet: "The intellect of man is forced to choose perfection of the life or of the work," or those of David Hull: "The behavior that appears to be the most improper actually facilitates the manifest goals of science. . . . As it turns out, the least productive scientists tend to behave the most admirably, while those who make the greatest contributions just as frequently behave the most deplorably." In other words, aggressiveness and selfishness are associated with superior performance by scientists.[5]

But our experiences and observations of eminent economists do not provide support for these assertions. In the case of our subject, Paul A. Samuelson, not only does he know how to maintain a balance between scholarship, family, and play, but he exhibits a high degree of humanity and kindness. The term *mensch* aptly describes him.

Samuelson blends childlike wonder with the extraordinary wisdom of experience, by continually challenging himself anew. For him, writing is synonymous with life, but never eclipses it. To paraphrase philosopher Martin Buber, the job is to drive the ploughshare of normative principles into the hard soil of positive economics. In this, Samuelson elegantly succeeds.

Acknowledgements

OUR GREATEST DEBT of gratitude goes to Paul A. Samuelson himself. His inspiration and wisdom continues to be a positive influence on our lives. We are particularly grateful for the time he spent meeting with us.

To supplement our material, we spoke and corresponded with a number of Samuelson's colleagues and past students, many of whom now occupy the front ranks of the economics profession. They provided us with impressions and anecdotes that substantially elevated our work. For their generosity and wisdom, we are deeply grateful.

A number of our dear friends and colleagues generously gave of their time to read drafts of this book. We would like to thank Mary Ellen Benedict, James Bradley, Alan Brown, Kristine Chase, Patrick Corrigan, John Golden, Abraham Goldstein, Paul Grimes, Patrick O'Neil, Allan Persky, and Peter Sperling.

Also, we would like to thank R' Hershel Maiman for his kindness, uncommon wisdom, knowledge, and generosity.

Deep gratitude and thanks are owed to the members of the Executive Board of Omicron Delta Epsilon, the Honor Society in Economics, for being a source of support: Professors Mary Ellen Benedict, James Bradley, Kristine L. Chase, Robert R. Ebert, William D. Gunther, Shirley Johnson Lans, Charles F. Phillips, Jr., and Robert S. Rycroft.

Our heartfelt gratitude to our assistant, Amelia B. Lacey, for her admirable overall skills, Charleston warmth, attention to detail, and friendship.

The librarians of Pace University—Adele Artola, Elizabeth Birnbaum, Amerne Denton, Michelle Fanelli, Alicia Joseph, and Sanda Petre—were unfailingly enthusiastic and supportive.

Thanks also to Tamara Kelly, Nicola Simpson, Katerina Soroka, and Carmen Urma for steadfast support, zest in work, and friendship.

The dedication of Jorge Pinto to bringing this book from idea, to manuscript, to printed page is gratefully acknowledged. He shepherded and championed our work. To say thank you is inadequate. Still, we say it. Thank you Jorge. We have also benefited from the comments of Kira Brunner, our wise, sympathetic, and demanding editor. Many thanks also to them both for an enthusiastic response to the text that brought out a perfect glint of joy in our eyes.

For various acts of kindness and assistance, we would like to thank Dr. Joseph Morreale, the Provost of Pace University, who brings a new vision to the University and to Lubin School of Business.

To all of you—our friends who cheered us on—our love is extended. It couldn't have happened and wouldn't have mattered without you.

How insightful of Winston Churchill to observe: "Writing a book is an adventure. To begin with, it is a toy and an amusement, then it becomes a mistress, and then it becomes a master, and then a tyrant."[6] The process of writing this book, however, was all joy for us.

Introduction

THE TREE in the Garden of Eden, the Kabbalists tell us, had ten branches, each of them endowed with special powers to open ten heavenly gates. One of those gates leads to creativity. Paul A. Samuelson, we would venture to say, doesn't need any keys to walk through the gate of creativity.

What is amazing about Samuelson is that, despite his advanced age, his life's work continues. What trumpet player Clark Terry stated of Duke Ellington applies equally well to Samuelson, "He wants life and music to be always in a state of becoming. He doesn't even like to write definitive endings to a piece. He'd often ask us to come up with ideas for closings, but when he'd settle on one of them, he'd keep fooling with it. He always likes to make the end of a song sound as if it's still going somewhere."[7]

We are drawn to thinkers, musicians, and scientists who are in a constant state of becoming. When Pablo Casals, the famous cellist, was asked why he continued to practice four hours a day at the age of ninety-three, he said, "Because I think I can still make some progress." Thus, we write of Paul A. Samuelson with an attentive eye but not with a dispassionate demeanor.

In contrast to the natural sciences, where Isaac Newton and Albert Einstein made their major contribution, most economic masterpieces were written when the authors were past middle age. For instance, Adam Smith, Karl Marx, John Maynard Keynes, and Milton Friedman all wrote their masterpieces when they were above middle age.

However, Samuelson started much earlier, in his twenties; and, at ninety, his articles are still influencing the field of economics and finance.[8]

Our objective in this book is twofold: first, to analyze and celebrate the achievements of Paul A. Samuelson during his legendary career—a career that continues today; second, to introduce the field of economics to sophisticated, yet non-economist readers, to provide a sense of the excitement and importance of economic debates during the twentieth century. To facilitate this broad audience, we strive to present ideas in an understandable, non-technical, and non-mathematical fashion—an endeavor that is often difficult.

We begin this book with a glimpse at Samuelson's early life. In Chapter 1, our emphasis is less on Samuelson's genetic background as it is on the "family" of economists he acquired during his education and career. In other words, we focus on nurture more than nature. Whether either truly matters is debatable. As Kenneth Arrow notes, "One might suppose . . . that the personal histories and class backgrounds of economists would be important factors. Yet, that does not seem to be the case. Among the great economists of the nineteenth century, David Ricardo was a highly successful businessman, a stock exchange speculator to be exact, while John Stuart Mill was brought up to be an intellectual by an exacting father. Yet, their economic theories were very similar indeed."[9]

We trace his life story, focusing heavily on his education at the University of Chicago and Harvard University. We take you to his first economics course at Chicago, taught by Aaron Director, and explore the "Chicago School" of economics. We introduce you to Jacob Viner's graduate course in economic theory, where the Samuelson "legend" began. And we learn about some of Samuelson's fellow students at Chicago, including the Nobel prize-winning economist Milton Friedman.

From Chicago we follow Samuelson to Harvard, and learn not only how Harvard made Samuelson, but how Samuelson, along with his fellow students, famously "made Harvard." We follow Samuelson through his participation in Harvard's Society of Fellows, and the completion of his famous Ph.D. thesis. We explore why Samuelson left Harvard for the Massachusetts Institute of Technology—a loss Harvard later regretted, but was never able to reverse.

In Chapter 2, we turn to Samuelson's philosophy and contributions to theory. We explore the factors that initially drove and sustained Samuelson's interest in economics. We analyze how Samuelson interprets his ideology of "overcoming inequality," his approach to the "equality versus efficiency" tradeoff, and why he advocates a "mixed economy." We then turn to his contributions to economic theory, beginning with a review of modern economics up to the *Keynesian Revolution*. We review some of Samuelson's contributions, including his approach to Keynes and his debates with Milton Friedman.

In Chapter 3, we explore what many consider Samuelson's most important contribution to economics: his methodology; specifically, his emphasis on mathematics. We vigorously argue that mathematics is an important tool in economics—though we recognize that it is a topic that terrifies most people unfamiliar with mathematics. We argue that this fear is due to poor "language" skills, the language to which we refer being mathematics. But once the "symbols" and "grammar" associated with the language of mathematics is understood, its precision, logic, existing concepts, and its ability to describe infinite dimensions make it the most efficient language for economists. We explore the nature of Samuelson's contributions to the application of math to economics, how it differs from his predecessors', and the controversies that resulted. We conclude Chapter 3 by distinguishing between theoretical and empirical economics, Samuelson's approach to each, and how he focused on empirical relevance—allegiance to the facts—instead of utopian ideas.

In Chapter 4, we consider various aspects of Samuelson's celebrity. We first look at Samuelson's textbook, *Economics*, and the renown it attracted. But we also take a close look at the criticism it generated as well—criticism, we shall see, that began before *Economics* was even published. We will introduce you to critics from the right and left, looking at everything from the book *Anti-Samuelson* to the critic that notoriously listed the 100 "heresies" of Samuelson. After considering a defense of *Economics*, we more lightheartedly conclude Chapter 4 with a look at "the spoils of battles"—namely, some of the more important awards and honors that Samuelson received during his career, including the Nobel Memorial Prize in Economics.

In Chapter 5, we provide two personal recollections of Paul Samuelson, from Avinash Dixit and Lawrence R. Klein; and, in the appendix, we provide some of Samuelson's sayings.

Chapter 1: Samuelson's Early Journeys

Let others praise ancient times;
I am glad I was born in these.
–Ovid

PAUL A. SAMUELSON was ubiquitous in twentieth century American economic culture — he was a policy maker, a columnist for *Newsweek Magazine,* and renowned for the many editions of his famous textbook, *Economics.* Yet, few today outside of the economics field understand why, when the Prize Committee searched for the economist most deserving of the second Economics Nobel in 1970, they chose Paul Samuelson from among a huge pool of potential awardees; or why it was Paul Samuelson that John F. Kennedy called upon for advice when shaping economic policy. Almost all celebrity diminishes with time, and rightly so; each generation has its icons, champions, and villains. Yet, Samuelson, who celebrates his ninetieth birthday in 2005, is more than a passing fancy — he remains relevant today. For Paul Samuelson is an economist's economist, whose approach to economics inspired change in the prism through which economists view their field. In this book we will probe the intellectual contributions of Samuelson, both to economic thought and methodology. Before doing so, however, this chapter will probe the early journeys of Samuelson as he developed into an American icon. Let's begin by taking a look at Samuelson's education, including the teachers, col-

leagues, students, and events that influenced his thinking
and his philosophy toward life and economics.

First Steps

PAUL SAMUELSON was born on May 15, 1915 in Gary,
Indiana. This small city seems to instill a passion for
supply and demand curves and academic paper writing,
for Gary produced several celebrated economists, including Samuelson's own student and fellow Nobel Laureate
Joseph Stiglitz. Stiglitz quips that something in the air in
Gary leads one into economics. Stiglitz also notes that
Samuelson describes him as the "best economist from
Gary, Indiana." Samuelson clearly has significant affection
for his hometown, teasing, "Gary is a good place to come
from (and so is the University of Chicago in economics)."[10]
But Samuelson was born into troubled times. On May 7,
1915, only eight days before Samuelson's birth, a German
U-boat torpedoed the ocean liner RMS *Lusitania*, which
was en route from the United States to Great Britain. This
attack, which killed 1,198 on board including 128 Americans,
strongly influenced the entry of the United States into
World War I in 1917.[11]

The demand for products during WWI resulted in an
increase in productive capacity — a skyrocketing demand
for goods is one of the dubious silver linings typically associated with the horrors of war (a fact not lost on conspiracy
theorists everywhere). When WWI ended in 1918, there
was a steep drop in demand for goods, straining economic
progress. Wages stagnated relative to growth in productivity.
The fruits of increased productivity flowed to the accounts

of investors instead of laborers. This unequal distribution of wealth was not only unfair, it foretold a serious fault within the American economic system as the failure of wages to grow undercut the ability of the American consumer to purchase products. During the mid 1920s, construction levels dropped, followed by a drop in automobile production. At the same time, deflation had a negative effect on those in debt, particularly those who borrowed money to finance farms. As food prices fell, farmers struggled, and often failed, to meet their interest obligations with their depressed cash inflows.

These factors, among other domestic and international factors, including a weak banking structure, the foreign balance of payments, and decreases in the money supply, all contributed to the period known as the Great Depression. The Great Depression "officially" began on October 24, 1929, when Samuelson was fourteen years of age. The stock market crash on this date, infamously known as "Black Thursday," was startling; yet, the much deeper subsequent decreases in stock prices, as well as vast unemployment, are among the most troubling aspects of the Great Depression.

It was during this era that Samuelson grew up, a period where reality suggested that the existing solutions to economic problems were inadequate. Samuelson's father owned drugstores, first in Gary and later in Chicago. Samuelson describes his family background as middle class. "Usually when you have a scholar of some distinction, he turns out to be descended from a long line of rabbis. I don't know what happened further back, particularly since my mother always had some delusions of grandeur about her lineage. But as far as I know, this has no justification at all, except that her grandfather, who came to this country before the Civil War at the time of the Gold Rush, got a nest egg that put her family a little higher in the social scale. By miscalculation, he went back to Europe—to that part of Poland that abuts East Germany."[12]

His parents were liberals. Says Samuelson, "I used to read on our family bookshelves books which my father, I guess when he was a bachelor, had acquired, many of them in used bookstores in Chicago, such as debates [of] Clarence Darrow on pacifism and religion and so forth." Noting his father's interest in such left-leaning figures as Darrow, Samuelson concludes, "I was reasonably inclined to be New Dealish before there was a New Deal."[13] Samuelson was educated in the Gary and Chicago public school systems, and graduated from Hyde Park High School. He fondly recalls his Hyde Park mathematics teacher Beulah Shoesmith, whom he describes as a "real terror of the old school."[14]

Samuelson entered the University of Chicago at the precocious age of sixteen in 1931. At that time Chicago housed one of the most important economics departments in the world. Samuelson describes his attending Chicago as a chance of geography—and indeed, the University of Chicago was within walking distance of his home. "In those simple days of the Depression," recalls Samuelson, "you went to college near your home, or to your father's college. My father had gone to pharmacy college, and his last wish was to have any of his three boys become a pharmacist. So I went to the University of Chicago."[15]

During his undergraduate studies at Chicago, Samuelson had the opportunity to learn from many leading economists—at "the best Department of Economics in the country."[16] Among the faculty were Frank H. Knight, one of the founders of the Chicago School; Henry Simons, Knight's student and an early Monetarist; and Paul Douglas, the economist-turned-politician who later became a U.S. Senator from the state of Illinois.

As a freshman Samuelson took an introductory course in economics taught by Aaron Director. It was this course that first activated Samuelson's interest in economics. "I walked into my first economics class," says Samuelson, "because I hoped to learn how not to go broke in the stock market as so many people were then doing. But I stayed for the second lesson to learn how my generation could avoid great depressions, like that of 1929–1935, which was causing my Midwestern neighbors to lose their savings at a time when thousands of American banks were failing."[17] Aaron Director was a strong libertarian who advocated that the government should play a very limited role in the economy. This was not an uncommon perspective at the University of Chicago, which was permeated by the *laissez faire* approach of neoclassical economics. The advocacy of libertarianism and neoclassical economics at the University of Chicago was so strong that this approach to economics is widely designated the "Chicago School" of economics. But given the state of the economy during this period, *laissez faire* was rapidly losing advocates. This was especially due to the economic prescriptions being written by John Maynard Keynes, who generally advocated heavy government intervention and whose seminal *General Theory of Employment, Interest and Money* was only a few years away from publication.

And then there was Professor Jacob Viner. "There has never been a greater neoclassical economist than Jacob Viner," wrote Samuelson.[18] And to this we add that it may also be true that there was never a more disquieting teacher. Though still only a senior and an undergraduate, Samuelson audited an important graduate course: Jacob Viner's graduate course in economic theory. Viner's course was a terrifying experience for any student. Viner implemented a three-strikes-and-you're-out policy, where failure to respond correctly to three of Viner's pointed questions resulted in exile from the course — typically followed by a swift change of career. No wonder he was known as "the chief and unavoidable ogre."[19] But our nineteen-year-old Samuelson, who didn't really belong in this graduate course in the first place, made his mark. Given that Samuelson was just an undergrad, and given Viner's perceived ferocity, his position in Viner's course should have been unassuming. Instead just the opposite was true. Samuelson was legendarily brash, and developed quite a reputation due to his habit of correcting Viner's blackboard errors. The stories of Samuelson's behavior as a young man grew over the years into the stuff of legend; to the point where Samuelson had to set the record straight following Viner's passing. "Fools rush in where angels fear to tread," Samuelson says self-deprecatingly, "and so it was left to the only undergraduate in the course to point out such occasional petty aberrations."[20] Fair enough. But this was also the beginning of a trend — where others feared to tread, Paul Samuelson frolicked.[21]

Samuelson was a celebrity even as an undergrad — recognized by both students and faculty. Martin Bronfenbrenner, the well-known economist and Samuelson's fellow student, recalls, "most impressive of all was Paul Samuelson, still technically an undergraduate and somewhat younger than myself, but well on his way to becoming the Liszt or the Paganini of twentieth-century economic gymnastics."[22] It's no wonder that Paul Douglas, one of Samuelson's mentors, felt he had to comfort other economics students through advising, "You needn't be as good as Samuelson to get along in economics."[23] Samuelson remains as sharp today. Bengt Holmstrom of MIT recalls a dinner at his house for a group of young faculty members, which Samuelson attended as well. "Prof Samuelson was there enjoying the young company. Between meals I arranged a light, informal trivia competition. Had answers been counted, the eighty-eight-year-old professor would have won hands down. He even knew the third president — of Finland — a question I threw in as a joke"[24]

Among Samuelson's fellow students, though at the graduate level, were future Nobel laureates and future pillars of the Chicago School George Stigler and Milton Friedman. Another economics Nobel laureate, Herbert Simon, also studied at the University of Chicago during this time. Friedman, who later went on to complete a Ph.D. at Columbia University, was a strong advocate of free markets in the tradition of the Chicago School. Yet, while attentive to the Chicago School perspective, Paul Samuelson was not convinced. As we will explore in Chapter 2, Samuelson's preference for the Keynesian approach was unbridled (at least originally).

As both of their legendary careers progressed, Samuelson and Friedman were often perceived as the two sides of the post-war economic story. For example, both wrote popular

articles for *Newsweek* magazine, Friedman representing
the conservative, libertarian perspective, and Samuelson
representing the liberal, Keynesian perspective.

LEAVING NIRVANA

IN 1935 SAMUELSON completed his undergraduate studies
and went on to graduate school at Harvard. The decision to
leave Chicago was not his: Samuelson was talented enough
to win a Social Science Research Council Fellowship, but
the fellowship came with the condition that his graduate
work could not be completed at the University of Chicago.
"Given my way," says Samuelson, "I would have stayed at
Chicago forever. Why leave Nirvana?"[25] The decision to
study at Harvard was not an obvious one: everyone urged
him to commence his graduate work at Columbia. So
why did Samuelson choose Harvard instead of Columbia?
"Truth to tell, it was because I expected Harvard to be
like Dartmouth—located around a New England green
common, with a white chapel tower and much ivy on the
walls."[26] Samuelson had a "naïve notion that Cambridge,
Massachusetts would be a peaceful green village where book
learning could explode."[27] So off to Harvard he went.

Samuelson describes Harvard's Department of Economics
in 1935 as "just moving from torpor into an Elizabethan
renaissance."[28] The "renaissance" of which Samuelson
speaks was due to the arrival of a number of academics
from Europe—exiles looking to escape a Europe on the
brink of exploding into World War II. These academics
included Joseph A. Schumpeter and Gottfried von Haberler.
Schumpeter facilitated the hiring of Wassily Leontief, an-

other future Nobel Laureate. Leontief taught a one-semester mathematical economics seminar—ostensibly a price theory course. "No other course I ever took so profoundly set me on the way of my life career"[29] was Samuelson's evaluation of the class. Other teachers from whom Samuelson benefited at Harvard University were Edwin Bidwell Wilson and Alvin Hansen. Samuelson describes Hansen as the "American Keynes."[30] And about Wilson, Samuelson writes, "I was perhaps his only disciple," and speaks glowingly of Wilson's contempt for "social scientists who aped the more exact sciences in a parrot-like way."[31]

But Samuelson's Harvard experience cannot be fully characterized in terms of his teachers alone—Samuelson speaks fondly about his fellow graduate students as well. No teacher's pet, Samuelson truly was one of the boys. "Contemporary Harvard graduate students came to match in brilliance the new Harvard faculty." Samuelson wrote in his essay "How I Became an Economist," "Richard Musgrave, Wolfgang Stolper, Abram Bergson, Joe Bain, Lloyd Metzler, Richard Goodwin, Robert Triffin, James Tobin, Robert Solow—all of them my pals—became the 1950–2000 era stars in world frontier economics. Harvard made us, yes. But as I have written many times, we made Harvard."[32] All went on to become accomplished economists. Tobin and Solow were future Nobel Laureates, receiving the prize in 1981 and 1987, respectively. Stolper was Samuelson's collaborator and friend, both residing on Ware Street, within walking distance of Harvard Yard. The mutual respect between Samuelson and Bergson, another friend and collaborator, whom he first met in Leontief's economics seminar, is noteworthy. "Leontief's seminar was small," Bergson recalled before his passing, "and a not so incidental attraction that it had for me was that Paul A. Samuelson attended it."[33]

Samuelson completed his M.A. at Harvard University in 1936, and received his Ph.D. in 1941 at the age of twenty-six. The five year long duration between Samuelson's M.A. and Ph.D.—atypical, that is, by his ambitious standards—was due to his appointment to Harvard's Society of Fellows in 1937. The Society of Fellows, founded as Harvard's alternative to its Ph.D. programs, provided students the opportunity to pursue any research that interested them for a three year period, with the condition that they were prohibited from working on their Ph.D. dissertations. Cofounder Abbott Lawrence Lowell, President of Harvard until 1933, believed that Ph.D. degrees "smothered creativity under a mountain of requirements."[34] Another cofounder, Lawrence J. Henderson, explained that the purpose of the Society of Fellows was "to provide an alternative path more suited to the encouragement of the rare and independent genius."[35] Ironically, Samuelson notes that his dissertation was "written mostly as a Junior Fellow."[36] Samuelson benefited greatly from participation in the Society of Fellows, describing it as a "veritable heaven."[37] It was during this period that he published several important academic papers. "I was a young man in a hurry," wrote Samuelson, "because I felt the limited life time of my male ancestors tolled the knell for me."[38] The passing of Samuelson's father, when Samuelson was only twenty-three years of age, intensified this sense of urgency.

Once the three-year restriction on pursuing a Ph.D. dissertation ended, mid-1940, Samuelson had a choice to make: should he write a formal Ph.D. dissertation? The decision was not obvious; Samuelson notes that several colleagues of his in the Society of Fellows were true to the purpose of the Society, and eschewed Doctorates. These include important leaders in their fields of study, including the founder of lattice theory in mathematics, George Birkhoff, among others. Samuelson notes "their Harvard careers never suffered from [not pursuing the Ph.D.]."[39] But Samuelson, encouraged by his wife, Marion Crawford Samuelson (with whom he would raise six children, including triplet boys![40]), now deceased, decided that he should write his Ph.D. dissertation, and it was completed quickly.

Samuelson's dissertation is one of the more important economics texts of all time. As the story goes, when Samuelson completed his defense of the doctoral dissertation, one member of the committee turned to another and said, "did we pass?" Winner of Harvard's David A. Wells Prize for best publishable thesis, it was published in 1947 under the title *Foundations of Economic Analysis.*[41] This text revolutionized the way that economists think about their field of study. Andrew W. Lo notes that Samuelson "assumed that individuals acted so as to maximize a quantity called 'expected utility.' . . . By modeling economic agents in this way, he hoped to be able to predict their behavior in much the same way that physicists predicted the behavior of physical objects. From that point on, virtually everything that we have done in neoclassical economics has followed suit. And there's no doubt that we have made enormous progress thanks to Samuelson—as Isaac Newton once said 'If I have seen further . . . it is by standing upon the shoulders of Giants.' "[42]

Samuelson later wrote that the work done in *Foundations* won him the Nobel Memorial Prize — not a shabby track record for a Ph.D. dissertation![43] But the following vignette, related to us by the distinguished University of Maryland economist, Thomas Schelling, best encapsulates the authority of *Foundations*. Schelling recalls, "In 1946 I was enrolled in Joseph Schumpeter's 'advanced theory' course at Harvard. Half way through the semester Schumpeter asked whether Mr. Schelling was in attendance. I raised my hand to identify myself, and Schumpeter embarrassed me by suggesting I correct him whenever he made a mistake. Everybody looked at me, as perplexed as I was. I later visited him at his office to find out what it was all about. He said that my response to an exam question, a few weeks before, had been so professional and so superior to anybody else's that he figured he could count on me to keep him straight. I couldn't tell whether he was serious. Then he asked me how I'd learned so much about dynamic stability conditions. I answered that I had read Samuelson's *Foundations*. He said, 'Oh.' "[44]

Interestingly, the story is told that Schumpeter was courting Marion Crawford as well. Despite Schumpeter's claim that not only was he the best economist, but also the best horseman and lover, Samuelson was the victor.

Samuelson's scholarship and incredible accomplishments during the completion of his Ph.D. dissertation were already creating quite a buzz in the world of Ivy League economics. Ostensibly, the soon-to-be-Doctor Samuelson was in a position to choose to join any institution following the completion of his graduate work. However, there was one Department of Economics at which the door of opportunity was effectively shut before him: Harvard. For instead of offering him a full time academic position, Harvard offered Samuelson the lower position of instructorship in the economics department—a position he begrudgingly accepted before going to MIT, not wishing to leave the Boston area. But how is it possible that Samuelson, who had already published several important papers, written *Foundations*, won the David A. Wells Prize, and was widely regarded as a *wunderkind*, found himself unable to obtain a full-time position at Harvard?

William Breit and Roger L. Ransom, in their book *Academic Scribblers*, argue that Samuelson was not offered a full time position at Harvard because "Samuelson's youth, brash personality, and Jewish background all worked against him."[45] The relationship between Samuelson and Department Chairman Harold Hitchings Burbank was particularly vitriolic. The David A. Wells Prize for best publishable thesis that Samuelson had received in 1941 required the Chairman of the Economics Department to publish *Foundations*. Yet, Samuelson tells of how Chairman Burbank initially directed that only 500 copies be published. After Samuelson objected, a first run of 750 was agreed upon. But Burbank continued to work against Samuelson. "His orders were to destroy all the beautiful mathematical type after the first run," Samuelson informs us. "When the first printing sold out immediately, all subsequent printings had to be done by photo offset."[46] Samuelson also recalls how Burbank counseled him "against working in economic theory before I had reached (his) ripe old age of 50+."[47] It is no wonder that Samuelson describes Burbank as standing for "everything in scholarly life for which I had utter contempt and abhorrence."[48] As it became increasingly clear that Samuelson had no future at Harvard, Samuelson accepted a position at the Massachusetts Institute of Technology (MIT), before completing his Ph.D. "I was not to get an early tenure offer from Harvard," writes Samuelson, "and, without malice, I revealed a preference for MIT. To everyone's surprise, including my own, that turned out to be the happiest decision of my life."[49]

MOVING UP, DOWNSTREAM

MIT IS ONLY three miles away from Harvard Yard, just downstream on the Charles River, with Boston University between the two. We would be derelict if we failed to include here what is likely Samuelson's most famous quote, in which he describes how "an *enfant terrible emeritus* packed up his pencil and moved three miles down the Charles River."[50] The friendly rivalry between Harvard and MIT is legendary.[51] Yet, Harvard's loss of Samuelson to MIT represents at least one occasion where MIT's triumph is unquestioned. Close to forty years later, Harvard still regretted its decision — as Otto Eckstein, the Harvard economist, put it in 1979, "Harvard lost the most outstanding economist of the generation."[52]

Samuelson is an icon to his students. As student and fellow Nobel laureate Joseph Stiglitz so elegantly puts it, "I often took Paul as a role model, the expansiveness of his learning, the breadth of his work, its originality and penetration. He wrote forcefully and beautifully."[53] Robert C. Merton, who was awarded the Nobel Memorial Prize in Economics in 1997, recalls a paper he coauthored with

Samuelson while working as his Research Assistant at MIT. The paper was to be presented at the inaugural session of the MIT-Harvard Mathematical Economics seminar in October, 1968. The crowd was high-powered, and included Kenneth Arrow, Wassily Leontief, and others of that intellectual caliber. Samuelson insisted that Merton present their paper, though Merton had never presented a paper at a formal seminar before. As Merton recalls, "it was surely a memorable baptism."[54]

Tony Atkinson of Oxford remembers his arrival at MIT. "I arrived as a visiting graduate student at MIT in September 1966, just off the boat from England, on a Saturday. My wife and I called at the Department of Economics to see if there was anyone working, and there was just one—Paul Samuelson, busy revising his textbook. Despite the imminent publisher's deadline, he made us most welcome, including providing tea, and it was a wonderful start to our year at MIT."[55]

Alan Blinder relates an anecdote from his doctoral days at MIT. "I arrived at MIT as a Ph.D. student in the summer of 1969. Miguel Sidrauski, a brilliant young monetary theorist, had died tragically a few months earlier, and the course listing said that Samuelson would teach what was supposed to have been Sidruaski's course in the fall semester. We all showed up on the appointed day, and found four upper-level graduate students sitting in the front of the room. It was quite a good group: Bob Merton, Jeremy Siegel, Karen Johnson, and Dave Scheffman. But we wondered why they were sitting in the front, rather than at desks, like us. Then Professor Samuelson walked in. He proceeded to tell us a story of how James Mill taught everything he knew to his oldest son, John Stuart, and then assigned John Stuart Mill the task of teaching his younger siblings. Transitioning to the present, he explained how these four fine graduate students had studied monetary theory the previous year, and would now teach us what they had learned. With that, he left the room and we never saw him (in that course) again!"[56]

Kenneth Rogoff of Harvard recalls his experience at MIT. "I was a graduate student at MIT in the late 1970s, and had the good fortune both to take a class from Paul Samuelson, and to interact with him one on one with questions about my thesis. Apart from the brilliance of his mind and the beauty of his writing, my strongest recollection is how much effort he put into getting to know mere mortals like me. He could, of course, lecture for an hour without interruption if no one dared ask a question. But if you did ask something, he would hone in on the question if he thought it worthwhile and not dodge it. Even a short trip to his office would spin off ideas that would keep you thinking for months. Samuelson set a standard in teaching and citizenship at MIT that few if any will ever match."[57]

Despite several attempts by Harvard's Department of Economics to woo Samuelson back to the fold, Samuelson remained at MIT for his entire career, receiving associate professorship in 1944, professorship in 1947, and Institute Professor — MIT's highest honor — in 1966.

Samuelson also contributed to the Second World War effort, as a staff member of the MIT Radiation Laboratory during 1944 and 1945, where he designed "automatic servomechanisms to ward off enemy bombers."[58] In plain English, Samuelson worked with a team devising techniques to track enemy aircraft. He was also a consultant for the National Resource Planning Board, and served on the War Production Board.

Samuelson remained loyal to MIT throughout his career, failing to be enticed by offers from Harvard as well as the University of Chicago, who tried to steal him from MIT in 1948. Chicago's interest in Samuelson was somewhat surprising considering that Samuelson's belief in a mixed economy didn't exactly square with the *laissez faire* philosophy for which the Chicago School was famous. But Theodore Schultz, then chairman of the Economics Department at the University of Chicago, wanted Samuelson as a counterbalance. Schultz's argument to Samuelson was enticing: "We'll have two leading minds of different philosophical bent — you and Milton Friedman — and that will be fruitful."[59] Samuelson tells us that he actually verbally accepted the offer initially, but changed his mind twenty-four hours later, fearing that the position would force him to counterbalance Friedman by adopting leftist opinions that he didn't fully agree with.[60] As we will discuss in greater detail in Chapters 3 and 4, Samuelson clearly defined himself as a centrist, rather than an advocate of a right- or left-wing philosophy and the fact that he was strongly criticized both from the left and the right attests to this. Samuelson also resisted presidential requests by John F. Kennedy and Lyndon B. Johnson to join the Council of Economic Advisers. As he said, "in the long-run the economic scholar works for the only coin worth having — our own applause. . . . This is not a plea for leaving the real world problems of political economy to non-economists. It is not a plea for short-run popularity with members of a narrow in-group. Rather, it is a plea for calling shots as they really appear to be, even when this means losing popularity with the great audience of men and running against the spirit of the times."[61]

Samuelson embraced the intellectual community at MIT, an act indicative of his philosophy that true fulfillment in economics flowed from trying to "stay informed on what other scientists have done and to advance the frontier by your own quantum jumps."[62] Samuelson strongly believes that one's intellectual environment is crucial. Samuelson argues, "There are very few great scholars working off by themselves with paper and pen far from the centers of creative economic thought. Those who pride themselves on being most autonomous usually end up most idiosyncratic."[63] Bengt Holmstrom recalls meeting Samuelson two weeks after first moving to MIT in the summer of 1994. "I saw Professor Samuelson in the hallway. His first question was: 'Have you noticed a significant increase in the rate at which you prove theorems after arriving to MIT?' It was his way of asking whether I found the intellectual atmosphere at MIT stimulating."[64]

Samuelson continues to represent an intellectual beacon of light to those with whom he comes into contact at MIT and elsewhere, whether colleagues or students. Indeed, three of his graduate assistants, Lawrence Klein, Robert Merton, and Joseph Stiglitz, and one of his students, George Akerloff, went on to win the Nobel Memorial Prize in Economics, attesting to Samuelson's influence. Jagdish Bhagwati of Columbia University (formerly of MIT), tells of Samuelson's astonishingly "genuine and deep interest in one's affairs with an equal readiness to engage in conversation on intellectual and economic questions."[65] Bhagwati recalls a reminiscence of Charles Kindleberger, the MIT economic historian and authority on international monetary affairs, who passed away in 2003. Kindleberger said that Paul Samuelson, the great theorist, always made him feel at home and was accepting of his non-theoretical approach. Bhagwati argues that this speaks to "both Samuelson's catholicism in interests and also to his immense generosity of spirit which his *enfant terrible* image concealed from many."[66]

Peter Temin, Professor of Economics at MIT, tells us of Samuelson's kindness: "When my brother won the Nobel Prize in 1975, my mother offered to take us all to Oslo. My wife, Charlotte, had been in an airplane fire some years before and not been willing to fly, but she made great effort to overcome her fear and go. That year was a big Nobel anniversary, and Paul [Samuelson] was going to Oslo with untold numbers of other Laureates. We were on the same plane from Boston — Paul in first class; we in economy. Paul came back from first class to sit near Charlotte and tell her an endless set of jokes and stories that kept her fear at bay for hours. It was a lovely act of friendship and kindness that we have never forgotten."[67]

Indeed, the evidence bears this out to be true. James Buchanan, who was awarded the Nobel Memorial Prize in Economics in 1986, tells us, "When . . . [Samuelson's] seminal 1954 piece on the pure theory of public expenditure was published, I had trouble with the basic logic. Samuelson was very helpful in getting me straight."[68] Lawrence R. Klein, who was awarded the Nobel Memorial Prize in Economics in 1980, described his experience after receiving a scholarship that allowed him to attend MIT following Berkeley. "There I met the dazzling *wunderkind* Paul Samuelson. When I was browsing in the Berkeley library and came across early issues of *Econometrica*, Samuelson's contributions caught my eye. When I got an opportunity to go to MIT, it was the possibility of working with Samuelson that confirmed all my choices. I was attached to him as a graduate assistant from the outset, and I tried to maximize my contact with him, picking up insights that he scattered on every encounter."[69]

But we don't mean to give the impression that Samuelson is pure sugar; he is known for spice, too. Jagdish Bhagwati tells us about one of Samuelson's encounters with the British economist, Thomas Balogh. Bhagwati recalls that when Samuelson "once traveled from Heathrow airport to a party in Oxford, he walked up to Tommy (later Lord) Balogh and said: 'Tommy, I have just been reading the *Financial Times* and I find that someone has signed your name to a terrible article; you must do something about it!' It left Tommy flabbergasted!"[70] Indeed, Samuelson's capacity for irreverence and wit is true to the John Maynard Keynes maxim: "Words ought to be a little wild for they are the assault of thoughts on the unthinking."[71]

ADDITIONAL NOTES AND SOURCES, CHAPTER 1

Our objective in this chapter is to provide some flavor of Samuelson's education, and the events that formed his perspective on life. The details are primarily based on Samuelson's own words, as well as the observations of his teachers, collaborators, colleagues, and students. The Nobel Foundation includes a nice biography of Paul Samuelson on its website, available at:

www.nobel.se/economics/laureates/1970/samuelson-bio.html

Other biographies include a chapter in William Breit and Roger L. Ransom's *Academic Scribblers* and K. Puttaswamaiah's "Contributions of Paul Samuelson," in Puttaswamaiah's *Paul Samuelson and the Foundations of Modern Economics*, among others. An excellent profile is the chapter on Paul Samuelson in Robert Sobel's *The Worldly Economists*.

Chapter 2:

Samuelson the Philosopher and Theorist

I want to be thoroughly used up when I die, for the harder I work, the more I live. I rejoice in life for its own sake. Life is no brief candle to me. It is a sort of splendid torch which I have got hold of for the moment, and I want to make it burn as brightly as possible before handing it on to future generations.
–George Bernard Shaw

SAMUELSON'S RESEARCH OUTPUT is legendary, as a quick perusal of the multiple-volume collection of his hundreds of papers can attest.[72] Samuelson's passion for his craft raises relevant questions: What was it that drew Samuelson's interest to economics as opposed to, say, science, mathematics, or even athletics? And what objectives sustain his interest? Samuelson's enthusiasm for economics was originally driven by an urge to satisfy his curiosity. And it didn't hurt that he was good—very good—at economic analysis. "I became an economist quite by chance," Samuelson tells us, "primarily because the analysis was so interesting and easy." Samuelson found economics so easy that he thought he was missing something. He recalls how "Prior to graduating from high school I was born again at 8:00 a.m., January 2, 1932, when I first walked into the University of Chicago lecture hall. That day's lecture was on Malthus' theory that human populations would reproduce like rabbits until their density per acre of land reduced their wage to a bare subsistence level where an increased death rate came to equal the birth rate. So easy was it to understand all this simple differential equation stuff that I suspected (wrongly suspected) I was missing out on some mysterious complexity."[73]

But it was not simply a quick ability that attracted Samuelson to economics. He was also motivated by a higher philosophical ideal. "Mine is a simple ideology that favors the underdog and (other things equal) abhors inequality."[74] Of course, such an ideology is not unique to Samuelson. The desire to overcome inequality is arguably the primary motivating consideration for many economists. Indeed, a surprisingly large proportion of early twentieth century economists (though not Samuelson) attribute their initial interest in economics to flirtations with Marxist thought, and its abortive solutions to inequality. And politicians and academics of all stripes repeat the "desire to overcome inequality" to the point of mantra. We are reminded of the legend of the leader who asked his flock in the middle of a lecture on the morality of charity, "if you had two fortunes, would you give one to the poor?" and received an enthusiastically positive response. "If you had two homes, would you give one to the poor?" Again the response was enthusiastically affirmative. But to the query, "If you had two coats, would you give one to the poor?" He received a surprisingly negative response. "I am confused," remarked the leader, "if you were willing to give away a fortune or a home to the poor, surely you would also give a coat? What is the difference?" The answer: "we don't have two fortunes, nor two homes. But two coats we have!"

Indeed, overcoming inequality is challenging. Strategies that reduce inequality often directly conflict with society's other objectives, such as increasing efficiency—the amount of output per unit of input; reducing inequality while striving for "the greatest happiness for the greatest number" is one of the supreme challenges that society faces. Samuelson is quite cognizant of these challenges. He advocates an approach that combines resolution of the "equality versus efficiency" conundrum with a "concern for the ethics of the outcome."[75]

As we discuss in Chapter 3, while Samuelson is both admired and blamed for increasing the rigor of mathematics' role in economics, Samuelson doesn't perceive economics as a pure science. Instead, Samuelson places economics somewhere between a series of value judgments and hard science, admitting that "our hearts do often contaminate our minds and eyes."[76] Samuelson once responded to an economist whose professed liberal leanings were not reflected in his writings by acerbically commenting, "I wondered how he knew he had a heart: it had been so long since he had used it."[77] It is fair to say that the war-induced booms and Great Depression busts that the economy experienced as Samuelson grew up influenced his thinking. Samuelson notes, "More important it was to see with my own eyes the First War's induced boom in the U.S. Steel-planned Gary, Indiana: East European workers were overjoyed to be able to work 12-hour shifts, seven days a week. I saw, too, and my family learned the hard way, how recession follows the boom the way sparrows used to follow the horse. Also, when I was age 10 and we lived in Miami Beach, Florida,

I experienced first hand what a real estate mania was like. And what it was like when the bubble burst."[78]

Yet, Samuelson's solution to inequality is not charity or an inattentiveness to improving efficiency. Instead, his solution is to maximize the degree to which disparate objectives can be satisfied in harmony. He has no problem with wealth, yet he advocates positions that worked against his personal economic interests. Samuelson notes that while advocating the closing of tax loopholes, he has no difficulty taking advantage of those that remain. Fundamentally, Samuelson represents a middle path between a "bleeding heart liberal" and a "selfish elitist," satisfying the Talmudic dictum that "men with vision walk in the middle."[79]

Interestingly, Samuelson attributes his appreciation of market forces to the abuses of the McCarthy era, as well as Nixon's enemy list, on which he was placed due to his criticism of Nixon's economic policies as a *Newsweek* columnist.[80] "McCarthy has a big effect on me. McCarthy, I think, was a near brush with fascism in this country. I don't know why, but Richard Nixon seems to me to have been a far brush. It might have gone further but it didn't."[81]

These events drove Samuelson to the right by leading him to conclude that the existence of many private employers instead of a single employer, such as the government, is crucial. He puts it this way: "when you are blackballed from government employment, there is great safety from the existence of thousands of anonymous employers out there in the market."[82] Samuelson is strongly critical of advocates of free markets who fail to enthusiastically defend personal freedoms and civil liberties. Samuelson recounts a lecture he delivered in the early 1990s at a New York area university to a group of sixteen academics and students. Samuelson asked the group whether they felt the actions of an individual mired in financial scandal at the time were wrong. Samuelson tells us that he was surprised to find that he was the only one to argue that the individual's actions were wrong.[83] Samuelson attributes the linkage between market and personal freedoms suggested in this criticism to his education at the University of Chicago, but admits to personally being less than convinced of the strength of this linkage. For while he is no fan of socialism, concluding that socialistic societies are neither freely democratic nor efficient producers, he also dreams of "a humane economy that is at the same time efficient and respecting of personal (if not business) freedoms."[84]

Samuelson advocates a "mixed economy," in which there are transfers between classes and individuals, hopefully to the benefit of all levels of society. While such transfers represent a constraint of individual autonomy, Samuelson does not perceive them as coercions per se. Instead, Samuelson argues that "redistributive welfare transfers are not coercions on people by an external State; but rather, in the fashion of John Locke and John Rawls, are part of a social contract in which each person, operating under a veil of ignorance concerning chance's draw for him/her, opts voluntarily to set up rules of the road designed by us to be binding to us."[85] Indeed, two recent studies show the admirable performance of mixed economies in Scandinavia in recent years.[86]

Richard Zeckhauser of Harvard tells us,

> While in college, I first saw Paul in person when he spoke to undergraduates. A question from the floor:

"So, Professor Samuelson, do you think the budget should ever be in balance?" Answer: "That reminds me of the tragedy of one of my classmates who never married. He remarked: 'When I was twenty-five it was fashionable for women to marry men who were thirty, but when I was thirty, it had become fashionable for women to marry men who were twenty-five.' But by Brouwer's Fixed-Point Theorem, I told him, there must have been a time." This, I have learned, is quintessential Samuelson — playful, leaping across boundaries, yet incisive.

I first got to speak with Paul when as a young economist I was invited to the MIT Economics lunch table. "Hello Professor Samuelson, I am Dick Zeckhauser." "Well I didn't think you were the vacuum cleaner salesman." Witty, playful, and even gracious in the Samuelsonian fashion. Paul and I played tennis a bit when he was in his sixties. His game style reflects his mental mindset. He is tricky with his sequence of shots, and he likes to cut off balls in the air, inside the baseline. We played pretty even, but of course he had the advantage of a quarter century's extra experience.

In recent years, Paul and I have mostly discussed decision theory, and finance in theory and practice. Yet, while Paul loves to study money, and ways to make it merely by understanding markets, one senses virtually no acquisitive instinct. Many years ago he set the problem of someone refusing a gamble once, but accepting it if he can experience that same gamble many times. Paul saw that such behavior was likely to be contrary to rational utility theory. Fifteen years ago, John Pratt and I worked out precise conditions for a closely related problem. My reward was to be bombarded with Paul's extensions and generalizations of this work ever since.

Paul's mind defies the physics outlawing perpetual motion. Sit next to him at a seminar, and he will be scribbling an article, perhaps one with mathematics, on a topic having nothing to do with the subject being discussed. And he is irrepressible in discussing the subjects that have caught his fancy. A few years back, I was flying to San Antonio. Arriving in Dallas for a transfer, I called my office: "Paul Samuelson called; it is important that you call him back." I did. Paul: "Hi Dick. I have a problem for you. Let's say you had a portfolio with two assets, A and B, and were allowed, ... How would your tolerance for risk . . . ?" I struggled my best to respond, knowing that with a few stabs in vaguely the right direction Paul would bound ahead to new insights. The conversation—on a subject that he was fluent in and I was struggling to comprehend—persisted for thirty minutes. "Paul, I am sorry, but I'm in the Dallas airport and have to catch a plane to San Antonio." I relaxed, knowing that his quick mind and vigorous enthusiasm had carried us through. "Oh, that's okay, just give me a call when you get to San Antonio." And I did. Perhaps a stray comment will serve as the grain of sand for one of his sea of pearls.

To know Paul Samuelson is to be engaged in a life-long intellectual conversation with the most important economist of our times, as well as with those he admires (and a few he does not). His ideas are generously distributed over a vast range of topics, with profound thoughts often dropped into an occasional phone call or chance meeting. Through his historical accounts, his personal stories, and his academic ruminations, he will also introduce you to his predecessors, including many he never met, his contemporaries, and many of his younger colleagues. He creates an exhilarating "You Are There" experience in the making of modern economics.[87]

Samuelson's dream society combines "economics with a heart" and "economics with a head." Unlike most dreamers, however, Samuelson strove to actualize these dreams through his copious academic and popular writing. Let's explore some of his contributions, in the context of modern economics.

A History of Economic Thought: Modern Economics and the Keynesian Revolution

We all face a similar reality: unlimited wants, but very limited resources. This reality most obviously applies to the poorest members of our society, whose wants include basics such as food and shelter. But it also applies to the richest members of our society, who may find that while their food and shelter wants are satisfied, other wants such as health, happiness, or a private airplane are not. Economists toil at identifying the processes through which humans choose to satisfy one want over another. And economists try to come up with methods through which more wants can be satisfied within the constraint of limited resources.

Economic theorists and philosophers trace the history of economic thought—the body of knowledge that has identified and tried to solve the problems of resource and want—thousands of years back.[88] Yet, they identify the past three centuries as the "modern" era of economics, an era characterized by new questions contemplated by scholars, new objectives, and new methodologies. The new questions arose as the world transitioned from centuries of feudalism—where serfs were obligated to the nobles, barons, and bishops who controlled feudal manors—to mercantilism, the system that predated the industrial revolution and the emergence of market economies. Under mercantilism, rulers strove to increase the wealth of the nation-states they controlled by increasing the amount of gold and silver in the national coffers. Rulers believed that by increasing exports and limiting imports, the size of their coffers could be expanded. This belief resulted in the implementation of policies such as import tariffs, heavy government regulation of the domestic market to ensure the products produced were ideal for export, and even the placement of constraints on domestic consumption. But the advent of mercantilism also led intellectuals to question whether such measures truly increase the wealth of the nation-state. And if not, what does? These questions led to deeper investigation, such as inquiries into the true definitions of wealth and value.

Simultaneously, the objectives that intellectuals strove to satisfy shifted from the well-being and wealth of rulers, the ascendancy of whom was typically perceived as being granted by a higher power and therefore unchallengeable, to a more egalitarian focus on the rights and well-being of the individual. The American and French Revolutions, in 1776 and 1789 respectively, exemplify these shifts—where for the first time in history, sovereignty rested with the people.[89] These societal changes were accompanied by post-Reformation acceptance of personal wealth accumulation.

The increased emphasis on personal rights and wealth resulted in an intellectual focusing on new objectives. The new methodologies that scholars used when attempting to tackle these objectives best characterize modern economics. These methodologies, which were inspired by the Scientific Revolution (associated with legendary scientists such as Nicholas Copernicus, Johannes Kepler, Galileo Galilei, and Isaac Newton), placed greater emphasis on mathematics and experimentation rather than on Aristotelian arguments.

Who were the first economists of the modern era of economics? Economists argue over this topic, but most trace the roots of the modern era of economics to a group of French intellectuals known as the *Physiocrats*, and to Adam Smith, a Scotsman who is widely known as the first classical economist. The *Physiocrats*, so named because they believed that economic behavior was driven by the laws of nature, or *physiocracy*, were heavily influenced by the ideas of philosophers such as John Locke and René Descartes. Their belief that the economy was driven by a natural order led them to argue against government intervention in the economy, a position that ran contrary to the approach advocated by supporters of mercantilism. Their position is best encapsulated in their motto, *laissez faire, laissez passer,* which means "let things alone, let them pass." Besides disagreeing with the mercantilists regarding government intervention, they also disagreed on the true source of wealth. It is not the amount of gold in one's coffers that creates a nation's wealth, the *Physiocrats* argued, but the amount of agricultural production net of consumption.

Adam Smith, who interacted with some of the *Physiocrats*, is best known for the text, *An Inquiry into the Nature and Causes of the Wealth of Nations*, published in 1776.[90] Agreeing with the *Physiocrats' laissez faire* philosophy, Smith amended their theory, contending that it is productive labor, rather than agriculture or gold, which is the source of a nation's wealth. He also argued that specialization, where one laborer focuses on a single task among the many required when manufacturing a product, is more efficient than a craftsman completing all of the tasks individually. These contributions, as well as his insights into the source of value and his distinction between "natural" versus "market" prices, are why many refer to Smith as the father of modern economics.

Adam Smith paved the way for a number of important English economists, including Thomas Robert Malthus, David Ricardo, James Mill, and his son John Stuart Mill. These economists made many important contributions. One notable example is Ricardo's theory of comparative advantage, put forth in his 1817 text, *The Principles of Political Economy and Taxation*. Ricardo argued that, even if a state can produce all products more efficiently than other countries, it is still worthwhile for the state to engage in trade with foreign states — indeed, all countries are better off engaging in trade rather than attempting to produce, regardless of production efficiency, all products domestically. How important is the theory of comparative advantage? Stanislaw Marcin Ulam, the famous mathematician who contributed to the Manhattan project, once asked Paul Samuelson to "name me one proposition in all of the social sciences which is both true and non-trivial." Samuelson's response, years later, was that the theory of comparative advantage fits Ulam's bill. Said Samuelson: "That it is logically true need not be argued before a mathematician; that it is not trivial is attested by the thousands of important and intelligent men who have never been able to grasp the doctrine for themselves or to believe it after it was explained to them."[91]

The theory of comparative advantage, like the concept of division of labor through specialization, was revolutionary, and drove progress in economic thought. Yet, these ideas were primarily focused on supply, whether supply of labor or manufactured products. A body of thought attributed to subsequent generations of economists, known as *neoclassical economists*, focused on demand issues as well. One example of the contributions of neoclassical economics is *marginal utility*—the idea that the value of a product is driven by the benefit that the consumer receives from the reception of an *additional* unit of the product, and not from the total benefit received from the product. For example, while we may perceive diamonds as valuable, a person in a desert perceives a thirst-quenching drink of water as more valuable. A related concept is the *law of demand*, which argues that the demand for a product is negatively related to its price.

Notable neoclassical economists include Leon Walras of France, William Stanley Jevons of England, Carl Menger of Austria, and Alfred Marshall (who some view as a classical economist), particularly for his 1890 textbook, *Principles of Economics*. As we mention in the next chapter, Marshall generally limited the mathematics in his text to footnotes, reflecting his perception of mathematics as less important than literary economic arguments. But his diagrams, such as the famous *Marshallian Cross*, which plots the intersection of an upward-sloping supply curve and a downward-sloping demand curve, represented an important consolidation of economic thought. Marshall was a professor at Cambridge University, and many of his students eventually became prominent economists in their own right. Among these students was John Maynard Keynes (1883–1946). Keynes' powerful intellect, and his 1936 text, *The General Theory of Employment, Interest and Money*, instigated yet another revolution in economic thought.

The Keynesian Revolution

This early twentieth century revolution was driven by realities that challenged the core beliefs of economists at the time. Earlier economists developed their ideas while assuming that markets were competitive. Yet, the American experience following the American Civil War during the 1860s suggested otherwise, with a few men capturing control of a huge proportion of American industry. These *robber barons* included widely recognized names, such as J.P. Morgan, Andrew Carnegie, Cornelius Vanderbilt, and John. D. Rockefeller, among others. Their existence required economists to rethink their entire approach toward economic problem solving. The crisis in economic thought was further exacerbated some sixty years later by the Great

Depression, which followed the "Black Thursday" stock market crash of October 24, 1929. The suffering that the populace experienced during this period, including huge increases in unemployment, suggested a failure of *laissez faire*, and a rethinking of the idea that the role of government should be limited.[92]

It is simply impossible to do justice to the Keynesian Revolution in a few paragraphs. Briefly, the accepted body of thought before Keynes (with a few exceptions) perceived unemployment as a temporary state, which would revert back to full employment equilibrium once wages adjusted to ensure supply met demand. Hence, the unemployed laborer would eventually gain employment, albeit at a lower wage level. The policy implication of these ideas was that companies should lower wages. This would allow them to employ more workers. These ideas were exemplified by a theory known as *Say's Law*. This theory, proposed by the classical economist Jean-Baptiste Say, argues that excess supply or demand cannot occur. This law is often summarized as "supply creates its own demand."

Keynes argued that the government should stimulate the economy through public works investment. The resulting increased employment would lead to increased demand, which would lead to more production, which would then lead to more employment. He referred to this impact of investment (spending) on the level of income as the *investment multiplier*. In 1930s, he adopted this concept that details how output rises (declines) following a rise (decline) in spending. His rejection of private industry as the sole source of investment in the economy — and his embrace of government — horrified advocates of *laissez faire*, but seemed to represent a reasonable solution to the severe unemployment during the Great Depression. These revolutionary ideas continued to reverberate, influencing public policy and leading to important debates among subsequent generations of economists, including Paul Samuelson. To Samuelson, "Economics itself was a sleeping princess waiting for the invigorating kiss of Maynard Keynes."[93]

ENTER SAMUELSON

SAMUELSON DESCRIBES the ease with which he made advances in economic thought, saying, "I have been blessed with an abundance of interesting problems to puzzle out. Many artists and writers run into long fallow periods when new creative ideas just will not come. Luckily, this has not been my problem."[94] Robert M. Solow, the MIT professor who was awarded the Nobel Memorial Prize in Economics in 1987, attributes much to the proximity of his office to Samuelson's. "MIT hired me primarily to teach courses in statistics and econometrics. In the beginning I fully intended to make my career along those lines. It did not turn out that way, probably for a geographical reason. I was given the office next to Paul Samuelson's. Thus began what is now almost 40 years of almost daily conversations about economics, politics, our children, cabbages and kings. That has been an immeasurably important part of my professional life."[95]

James Poterba tells us of his first week at MIT. He had

been hired as an instructor, with a not-yet-finished dissertation at Oxford that explored a number of

issues in taxation and corporate finance. One of
the chapters in my dissertation looked at the stock
market's valuation of a small public utility company
in Connecticut that had two classes of common stock.
One paid dividends in cash, the other paid dividends
in stock, and the difference offered an opportunity
to learn about how the stock market valued dividend
payouts on "ex-dividend days." There had been one
other academic paper about this firm, but to be sure,
it was a small and somewhat anomalous company.

The year was 1982, and MIT's faculty club was on
the top floor of the building where the Economics
Department was located. Sometimes, at the end of
the day, some of my senior colleagues would walk
upstairs for a drink. I was invited to join this group,
and Paul Samuelson was also part of it. When we
had our drinks, Paul pulled me aside, sat down alone
with me, and asked me to tell him about my research.
I was immediately struck that he was interested in
hearing about what the most junior member of the
department was doing—and I have seen Paul's efforts to reach out to newcomers to our department
and our profession many times since. For my part,
the prospect of explaining my not-yet-defended dissertation research to one of the most distinguished
economists of the century, one-on-one, was nothing
short of terrifying. But I plunged ahead and began to
explain that I was working on a study of the market
valuation of a small firm called Citizens Utilities.
Paul cut me off mid-sentence. "Now, that's the one
with the Class A and the Class B shares, right, and

the different dividend treatment, isn't it?" My terror turned to awe. I was thrilled that Paul was interested in my work, and astonished that his encyclopedic knowledge of economics extended to the minutiae of the particular company I was studying.

This first encounter has had a long-term effect on my interactions with Paul Samuelson during twenty-two years as his colleague. On many occasions, I have screwed up my courage and called on him to talk about my research, most often when it touched on some aspect of financial economics. I am no longer astonished by his encyclopedic knowledge of economics, but I remain thrilled by his interest in the ongoing research of so many of his junior colleagues in the economics profession.[96]

Samuelson's hundreds of academic papers are evidence of his brilliance. Samuelson contributed to our understanding of how public expenditures can be optimized in articles such as "The Pure Theory of Public Expenditure" (1954), "Diagrammatic Exposition of a Theory of Public Expenditure" (1955), and "Aspects of Public Expenditure Theories" (1958). He contributed to the understanding of the mechanism through which the price of the factors of production would be equalized. He developed the Factor-Price Equalization Theorem, in articles such as "International Trade and the Equalisation of Factor Prices" (1948), "International Factor-Price Equalisation Once Again" (1949), and "Price of Factors and Goods in General Equilibrium" (1953). Factor-Price Equalization Theory states that free international trade leads to equalization of factor prices, such as labor and capital, among the countries. The theorem was developed by two Swedish economists, Eli Heckscher and Bertil Ohlin, but only proven by Paul Samuelson in 1948. The Stolper-Samuelson Theorem, co-authored with Wolfgang Stolper in 1941, related real wages to trade restrictions.[97] The Stolper-Samuelson Theorem states that a relative rise in the price of one or two goods leads to a higher return for the factor of production more intensely used and a lower return for the factor of production less intensely used. In other words, an increase in the relative price of a good increases demand for the factors that produce that good, thereby increasing the return for those factors and lowering the return for those factors that produce other goods.

Samuelson's Revealed Preference Theory, presented in "A Note on the Pure Theory of Consumer's Behavior" (1938), is one of his most important contributions.[98] This theory mathematically demonstrates how relative preferences can be deduced from market choices. Revealed Preference Theory is an approach to demand theory based on actual choices made by consumers in reaction to changes in product prices and consumer income. The beauty of this method is that consumer choices are observable whereas preferences are not.

Samuelson also contributed heavily to finance theory, in articles such as "Proof that Properly Anticipated Prices Fluctuate Randomly" (1965), "Rational Theory of Warrant Pricing" (1965), "General Proof that Diversification Pays" (1967), "Lifetime Portfolio Selection by Dynamic Stochastic Programming" (1969), and "The Fundamental Approximation Theorem of Portfolio Analysis in Terms of Means, Variances, and Higher Moments" (1970). It is no wonder that Samuelson is recognized as one of the founders of modern finance.

The Le Chatelier principle explains how a system that is in equilibrium will react to a perturbation. It predicts that the system will respond in a manner that will counteract the perturbation. Samuelson, following the methods of the hard sciences, has transported this principle of chemist Henri-Louis Le Chatelier to economics, to study the response of agents to price changes given some additional constraints. In his extension of this principle, Samuelson uses the metaphor of squeezing a balloon to further explain the concept. If you squeeze a balloon, its volume will decrease more if you keep its temperature constant than it will if you let the squeezing warm it up.[99] This principle is now considered as a standard tool for comparative static analysis in economic theory.

Like many others, Laurence J. Kotlikoff of Boston University feels that Samuelson is the finest economist who ever lived. And when he introduced Samuelson this way at a talk, Kotlikoff recalls how Samuelson "proceeded to run his first finger in a circle around his head suggesting I was crazy to make that statement. But it's a fair statement. The fact that he pooh-poohed my accolade is testimony to his modesty and character, which comes across in his every conversation."[100] Martin Bronfenbrenner wrote in 1982, "Others in Samuelson's age group, perhaps, have equaled or even surpassed him in rigor or vigor, but hardly in both. Others, perhaps, have made roughly equivalent or superior contributions . . . but who among them, I wonder, has equaled Samuelson across the board? I consider Friedman and Hicks, Myrdal and Mrs. Robinson, and reluctantly shake my head, although others may well disagree. One must go back one generation, to the generation of Keynes and Schumpeter, or so it seems to me, to find Samuelson's equal among economists at once generalist and specialist in so many fields."[101]

Samuelson's most important contribution to the Keynesian Revolution is arguably his textbook, *Economics*, which presented Keynesian thought to generations of American and non-American economics students for the first time—a fact that made some unhappy, as we will see in the next chapter. In *Economics*, Samuelson developed original methods of conveying Keynes' ideas. For example, Samuelson's Keynesian Cross represented an easy-to-understand explication of problems, such as unemployment, that plagued the United States during the Great Depression—and suggested that government spending might be the solution. The Keynesian Cross graphically relates total spending to measurements such as the Gross Domestic Product (GDP). Due to Samuelson's advocacy of the use of government spending, he was categorized as a fiscal Keynesian in the same school of thought as one of his professors at Harvard, Alvin Hansen. And it was Hansen that Samuelson credits for one of his most important papers, "Interactions Between the Multiplier Analysis and the Principle of Acceleration," which extended Keynes' investment multiplier through introducing the accelerator principle.[102] The accelerator principle relates the rate of change of output to the rate of investment, demonstrating that a small change in output can lead to a much larger change in investment—a change that will eventually, nonetheless, plateau. The interaction of the multiplier and accelerator has been used to explain business cycles.

Interestingly, Samuelson prefers to call the Multiplier-Accelerator Theory the Hansen-Samuelson Model, to ensure Hansen receives credit. Samuelson recalls that Hansen used the model to argue "that the upswing of the 1930s was not a full-bodied recovery attributable to basic exogenous factors, but rather a temporary recovery attributable to the temporary investment induced by a transient rate of rise of consumption. Such a consumption recovery, he said somewhat ambiguously, will only go as far as it is pushed."[103] Samuelson explains his own contribution as follows: "It was a case of mathematics not as the Queen of the Sciences but as the Handmaiden of the Sciences. I took *Hansen's* model, recognized its identity to a second-order difference equation with constant coefficients, and proceeded to analyze its algebraic structure."[104]

The Keynesian Revolution stimulated Samuelson, as it did most economists. But as scholarship progressed, so too did Samuelson's thinking. Samuelson argues that, to him, "Keynesianism was never a religion. 'What have you done for me lately?' was always the battle cry. Besides, the American Keynesians . . . were evolving beyond Model T Neanderthal Keynesianism. I race along with the avant garde."[105] When a new movement developed that attempted to synthesize Keynesian and neoclassical thought into equilibrium models, known as the *neoclassical synthesis*, Samuelson embraced it as well. This new movement is attributed to the English economist John R. Hicks, the 1972 Nobel laureate, whose ideas were published as early as 1937.[106] These ideas became popular in American economic circles, somewhat belatedly, after Alvin Hansen presented them in his 1953 book *A Guide to Keynes*, with Samuelson following suit.

Indeed, Samuelson remarks that by the time Hicks received the Nobel prize in the 1970s there were very few "Keynesians" anymore. Samuelson notes: "Few of my MIT students will call themselves 'Keynesians' as Solow, Modigliani, and I might. They are 'neo-Keynesians,' 'neo-neo-Keynesians,' and even 'anti-Keynes Keynesians.' But make no mistake about it. Their writings and views are light-years away from the macro I learned at the University of Chicago. And the common core of their beliefs is scarcely country miles away from the vulgar IS-LM diagrammatics that Harrod, Hicks, and Hansen distilled out of Maynard's intuitive explorations."[107]

As Keynes' ideas were debated, and as historical events led many to criticize the solutions that Keynesians proffered, other movements gained followers. A prominent example is monetarism, a school of thought associated with the Chicago School of economics — particularly Milton Friedman, whose 1956 *Studies in the Quantity Theory of Money* generated interest in monetarism. The Chicago School's emphasis on monetary policy was perceived as a reasonable solution to the inflation problems that many attributed to Keynesian policies. Samuelson argues that the failure of the Keynesians can at least be partially traced to the politically controversial stance of raising taxes. "In part, the disenchantment came because of failures of Keynesian policies to stop the inflation of the 1970s. It appeared that Keynesian fiscal policies were effective at stimulating the economy but political resistance to raising taxes led to ineffectiveness against inflation; fiscal policies were all accelerators and no brakes. In addition, many macroeconomists believed that the Keynesian approach had underemphasized the importance of incentives for long-run economic growth. Finally, critics tended to think that Keynesians made too much of price and wage inflexibility and that self-equilibrating forces were relatively powerful."[108] While Samuelson agrees that the 1979 monetarist experiment led by Federal Reserve Chairman Paul Volcker did reduce inflation, he argues that there is a price to be paid for such policies.[109] "Numerous economic studies . . . suggest that the tough monetarist policy worked, but at a cost. In terms of unemployment and output losses, the economic sacrifices of the monetarist disinflation policy were about as large, per point of disinflation, as those of anti-inflation policies in earlier periods. Money works, but it does not work miracles. There is no free lunch on the monetarist menu."[110]

Samuelson didn't only disagree with Friedman about policy; they had different methodological approaches as well. One of the more divisive debates in economics is how to evaluate a theoretical model. The controversy between the two scholars erupted when Friedman argued that a "theory is to be judged by its predictive power . . . the only relevant test of the *validity* of a hypothesis is comparison of its predictions with experience."[111] To Friedman, the assumptions underlying the theoretical model don't have to be realistic. Instead, the assumptions have to represent "good approximations." And what allows us to judge an assumption as a good approximation? Says Friedman: "this question can be answered by seeing whether it yields sufficiently accurate predictions."[112]

Samuelson referred to Friedman's logic as the "F-Twist," which he defines as follows: "A theory is vindicable if (some of) its consequences are empirically valid to a useful degree of approximation; the (empirical) unrealism of the theory 'itself,' or of its 'assumptions,' is quite irrelevant to its validity and worth."[113] Samuelson strongly disagreed with Friedman. To him, the F-Twist "is fundamentally wrong in thinking that unrealism in the sense of factual inaccuracy even to a tolerable degree of approximation is anything but a demerit for a theory or hypothesis (or a set of hypotheses). Some inaccuracies are worse than others, but that is only to say that some sins against empirical science are worse than others, not that a sin is a merit or that a small sin is equivalent to a zero sin."[114]

To Samuelson, Friedman's approach can result in empirical problems: "abstract models are like scaffolding used to build a structure; the structure must stand by itself. If the abstract models contain empirical falsities, we must jettison the models, not gloss over their inadequacies. The empirical harm done by the F-Twist is this. In practice it leads to Humpty-Dumptiness. Lewis Carroll had Humpty Dumpty use words any way he wanted to. I have in mind something different: Humpty Dumpty uses the F-Twist to say, 'What I choose to call an admissible amount of unrealism and empirical invalidity is the tolerable amount of unrealism.' The fact that nothing is perfectly accurate should not be an excuse to relax our standards of scrutiny of the empirical validity that the propositions of economics do or do not possess."[115]

One illness that has unfortunately infected many academics is infighting and personal jealousies. Samuelson, even in his theoretical disagreements with Friedman, believed that, just as physicians must fight cancer and not each other, so too must economists pursue the "objective reality out there that we are trying to understand, hard as the task may be. If ever a person becomes sick to death of faculty intrigue and professional infighting, if ever one sees democracy and civilization crumbling around one, always one can retreat to that objective study of reality."[116] And Samuelson practiced what he preached. Samuelson modestly speaks of Friedman's more influential presence.[117] And Samuelson notes that Friedman and he were "able to identify the source and texture of our disagreements in a way that non-economists cannot perceive. . . . I could disagree 180° with his policy conclusion and yet concur in diagnosis of the empirical observations and inferred probabilities."[118] Samuelson and Friedman often disagree strongly, but they disagree in style. In a 1976 *Newsweek* article, following his winning of the 1976 Nobel Prize in Economics, Samuelson discusses Friedman: "The fact that he and I, despite our policy disagreements and scientific differences, have remained good friends over 40 years says something perhaps about us, but even more I dare to think about political economy as a science."[119]

Milton Friedman has kind words for Samuelson as well: "though Paul and I have often differed sharply on issues of public policy, we have been good personal friends and have respected each other's competence and contributions to economics. Paul described the situation very well in a comment in a letter of December 8, 1995: 'I hope it will be said of us that, though we disagreed on much, we understood wherein our logical and empirical differences were based and that we were pretty good at preserving amiability, friendship, and respect throughout.' "[120]

Friedman tells us, "Paul and I were subject to very much the same intellectual influences at the University of

Chicago. Both of us were much influenced by Jacob Viner, Frank Knight and Henry Simons; Paul also by Aaron Director, Rose's brother who was teaching when Paul was an undergraduate."

"In 1966, when Henry Hazlitt terminated his role as a regular columnist on *Newsweek*, the editors of *Newsweek* decided to replace him with a troika of columnists, choosing Paul Samuelson as a representative of the 'new economics' or 'New Deal' liberal wing of the profession; Henry Wallich as a representative of the large center, and myself as a representative of the 'old liberal' or 'free enterprise' wing. I was very uncertain whether to accept, and one of the things that finally persuaded me to do so was a long telephone conversation with Paul who strongly urged me to agree. For the next fifteen years, until Paul terminated his column in 1981, we both wrote a column once every three weeks and *Newsweek* proved to be an excellent base for both of us. We often disagreed on substance but at no time during that period was there any personal disagreement or any personal problem whatsoever. On the contrary, we were mutually supportive."[121]

ADDITIONAL NOTES AND SOURCES, CHAPTER 2

Samuelson's theoretical contributions are too numerous to summarize in a single chapter, or even a single book. Such a summary is particularly difficult without the use of mathematics, Samuelson's natural medium. Hence, please recognize that we simply attempted to provide the reader with a flavor of Samuelson's contributions in this chapter, without feigning to represent even a cursory summary. Due to limitations of space, only the most celebrated Western economists are surveyed in this book. We realize that any rendition of history is controversial. The great controversies regarding interpretation mean that almost every interpretation is debatable. Texts that influenced our interpretation include E. Ray Canterbery's *The Making of Economics*; Everett J. Burtt, Jr.'s *Social Perspectives in the History of Economic Theory*; Lewis H. Haney's *History of Economic Thought*; and, of course, Paul A. Samuelson and William D. Nordhaus' *Economics*, any edition. To learn more about Samuelson's research contributions, we suggest you read George F. Feiwel's *Samuelson and Neoclassical Economics*. The papers we highlight as examples of Samuelson's theoretical contributions are loosely based on a chapter in the book by Michael D. Intriligator, titled "The Contributions of Paul A. Samuelson to Economic Analysis: A Revealed Preference Approach." Of course, anyone seriously interested in reading Samuelson can't avoid reading his multi-volume *The Collected Scientific Papers of Paul A. Samuelson*.

Chapter 3: Samuelson's Method

I will maintain that the artist needs only this:
a special world of which he alone has the key.
—André Gide

AMONG PAUL SAMUELSON's many contributions to economic thought, his application of mathematics to economics is perhaps the most famous. Indeed, in the speech that announced Samuelson's Nobel Memorial Prize, Professor Assar Lindbeck of the Stockholm School of Economics singled out Samuelson's analytical and methodological contributions, before ever mentioning any of his specific contribution to theory. "Samuelson's contribution," Lindbeck said, "has been that, more than any other contemporary economist, he has contributed to raising the general analytical and methodological level in economic science. He has in fact simply rewritten considerable parts of economic theory. He has also shown the fundamental unity of both the problems and analytical techniques in economics, partly by a systematic application of the methodology of maximization for a broad set of problems."[122]

But let's be honest: most people are terrified of math, and mystified by economics. And when math and economics are combined, the potent results are about as incomprehensible and mind-numbing to non-economists as brain surgery is to the layman. But fear not, for our objective in this chapter is not to teach you mathematics (or, at least, not much), but instead to explain why mathematics is useful and important, and to explore the role that Paul Samuelson played in introducing mathematics into economics.

MATH AND ECONOMICS

ULTIMATELY, math is a language. As Samuelson observes, "In principle, mathematics cannot be worse than prose in economic theory; in principle, it certainly cannot be better than prose. For in deepest logic—and leaving out all tactical and pedagogical questions—the two media are strictly identical."[123] In other words, math is the language Samuelson used to write economic theory. But if math is a language, then one must understand the fundamentals of the language. You can't learn how to read, say, Japanese without a detailed understanding of the symbols and grammar associated with Japanese. Similarly, it is impossible to learn how to read most—if not all—theoretical economics without studying the symbols and grammar associated with the language of math.

Anyone who has successfully completed a few years of elementary education will be very familiar with many of the basic symbols (such as the Arabic numerals) and may be familiar with some of the grammatical rules (such as the rule that if you place the symbol "+" between the numbers two and three, then the phrase "2 + 3" is equivalent to the number five). But, as Alexander Pope wrote, a little learning is a dangerous thing. The limited mathematics one learns in school represents only a small proportion of the symbols and grammatical rules that are actually associated with the mathematics language. Many find economics confusing because they can't easily apply their limited math knowledge to the frightening math they find in economic writings.

An analogy can be drawn to the tourist who had learned a few phrases of French in high school visiting Paris. The tourist may know how *acheter une pomme sur le marché*, but would face grave difficulty appreciating *Les Misérables* in the original French. Luckily for those who do not speak French, *Les Misérables* now plays on Broadway in English. But to the best of our knowledge, no economics text has yet been turned into a musical; hence, much of economics remains unfathomable to a non-economist audience.

Given that math tends to make economics unpalatable to non-economists, why is economics so mathematical? After all, if mathematics is simply another language, why bother with it in the first place? The simple answer is that there are many features of the language of mathematics that make it a particularly useful language with which to describe economic concepts.

First, mathematics is precise; it permits the economist to describe complex concepts using simple symbols. This precision becomes more important when multiple concepts are being described at the same time. Of course, when the definitions of the symbols are not provided, the symbols themselves are completely useless. The poor economics student who walks into an economics class late one day, only to see

$$\frac{x_i}{x_j} = \left(\frac{a_i}{a_j}\right)^{1/(1-m)} \left(\frac{p_i}{p_j}\right)^{1/(m-1)} = \frac{f'(\phi)\dfrac{\partial \Phi}{\partial p_i}}{f'(\phi)\dfrac{\partial \Phi}{\partial p_j}}$$

scrawled on the chalkboard might as well walk right out. Unless these variables were previously defined, they have no meaning.[124] But, when the definitions of symbols are known, math allows the economist to precisely describe complex concepts. Mathematical symbols can convey more meaning in a smaller amount of time than words.

Second, when making an argument using mathematics, the economist is forced to clearly explain exactly how "*a* leads to *b*."[125] Any assumptions one makes must be clearly stated; mathematically manipulating symbols without stating one's assumptions will result in an immediate barrage of criticism. In forcing the economist to state assumptions up front, the applicability of the economic analysis to reality is more easily determined, and the implications of a change in assumptions can be rigorously investigated. Thus, mathematics takes much of the "sloppiness" out of economic thinking.[126]

Third, the existence of an extensive body of mathematical knowledge outside of economics means that the economist can plug an existing mathematical concept — or theorem — into an economic model, without having to rediscover the logic behind the math concept from first principles. To understand why this is important, imagine if every time you bought a computer, you had to hire a programmer to create all of the applications you use, such as a document editor, e-mail host, and Internet interface, from scratch. This would be very inefficient, time consuming, and expensive, to say the least! In reality, of course, this is almost never required. Instead, one can easily purchase programs that have wide applicability, and customize them for personal use. Similarly, an economist has a wide range of mathematical tools and proofs that can be applied to the specific economic problem that he or she is trying to solve.

Fourth, math has an important advantage over pictures or graphs. While a picture may be worth a thousand words, it is also limited to, at most, three dimensions (or four dimensions, using animation software).[127] But economic problems quite often have a multitude of dimensions. For example, consider an economist who wants to model the process through which an individual consumer makes the relatively mundane decision to "go shopping." Many factors can influence one's decision to go shopping, such as the size of one's bank account, the weather, the time of day, the proximity of the shopping center to one's home, the availability of a car, the sitcoms on T.V., and so on. Using a single picture to describe the interaction of so many factors is simply impossible; a mathematical equation, on the other hand, can describe a large — or even infinite — number of factors.

Once you learn the language of mathematics, even heavily mathematical economics becomes understandable. Samuelson noted that his friend Nicholas Georgescu-Roegen argued, in relation to a particularly tricky economic issue, that "it is impossible to state such complicated mathematical relations in mere words." Samuelson disagreed with this assertion stating instead that "mathematics is language and in principle what one fool can comprehend so can another."[128] You cannot be exposed to Samuelson for long without getting a taste of his humor.

Samuelson was not the first economist to apply mathematics to economics. Leon Walras, one of the *Marginalist Revolutionaries*, applied mathematics heavily to economics, as did Alfred Marshall and still others. Yet, Samuelson's use of mathematics differs from most of his predecessors.

The best way to explain this difference is to draw out the distinctions between their uses of mathematics. Many contrast Marshall's use of mathematics to Samuelson's. This is likely because Marshall, similar to Samuelson, was an author of a popular economics textbook, *Principles of Economics.* Marshall, who was well educated in mathematics, generally relegated the mathematics in his text to footnotes, reflecting his perception of mathematics as less important than literary economic arguments. Samuelson's approach was the opposite; he used mathematics to extract insight that could only be gleaned through analyzing the wider picture provided by mathematics, and that could not be understood using intuition alone. The economist Robert Dorfman expressed a sentiment similar to this philosophy when he wrote, "I propose that mathematics is the technique of expressing relationships, usually symbolically, in such a way as to bring out their formal structure and then taking advantage of accumulated knowledge about the properties of such formal structures to reveal further relationships which are not immediately evident. The advantage of this procedure is its enormous economy."[129]

In his introduction to *Foundations of Economic Analysis,* Samuelson presents the following dictum of Marshall's: "it seems doubtful whether any one spends his time well in reading lengthy translations of economic doctrines into mathematics that have not been made by himself." Samuelson strongly disagrees. For, although it was true that when he began writing *Foundations* he "hoped that the discussion could be made non-technical," he discovered that "very quickly it became apparent that such a procedure, while possible, would involve a manuscript many

times the present size."[130] Regarding Marshall's critique of
those who use mathematics to present economic concepts,
Samuelson writes that this criticism "should be exactly
reversed. The laborious literary working over of essentially
simple mathematical concepts such as is characteristic of
much of modern economic theory is not only unrewarding
from the standpoint of advancing the science, but involves
as well mental gymnastics of a peculiarly depraved type."
To be fair to Marshall, his approach is reflective of the economic environment of his era. Alan Blinder notes, "There
is little doubt that economics circa 1900 was not a science.
Peruse copies of the leading economics journals around
the turn of the last century, and you will find articles
with titles like 'The Anthracite Miners' Strike of 1900.' In
other words you will find an almost complete absence of
equations. And, of course, you will find no regressions
or statistical hypothesis testing of any kind—the main
techniques having not yet been invented. More generally,
you will find little in the way of what I take to be the
hallmark of science: formulating theoretical models and
confronting them with facts."[131]

And Samuelson practices what he preaches. He has been
known to abbreviate earlier literary economic theories by
translating them into mathematics. In 1954, Samuelson
published a paper in the *Review of Economics and Statistics*
titled "The Pure Theory of Public Expenditure."[132] This
paper is notable among Samuelson's numerous publications because it restated, in only two and a half pages of
mathematics, important earlier insights into public finance.
More generally, Assar Lindbeck notes that "It is hardly an
exaggeration to say that he single-handedly rewrote con-

siderable parts of central economic theory: microeconomic theory, static and dynamic, partial and general equilibrium theory, as well as welfare economics. By extracting interesting inferences from simple mathematically formulated models, exploiting effectively the second-order conditions of maximization procedures, he derived results which today still rank among the classical theorems of economics."[133] Frank Hahn, a professor of economics at Cambridge University, describes a 1956 stint as visiting professor at MIT. "Not only was Samuelson by far the cleverest and most versatile economist I had ever met," recalls Hahn, "but he disposed of a wide and vast intellectual capital. He taught me the great economist's art of how to reduce a messy and difficult problem to manageable size."[134]

In the same issue of the *Review of Economics and Statistics* that published Samuelson's two and a half pages of mathematics, a "slugfest" raged over the role of mathematics in economics. An economist from the RAND Corporation, David Novick, launched the first attack, writing, "the richness of social science today arises chiefly from the stimulus to thinking which follows from the fact that little or nothing in the theorems now used is susceptible to absolute proof; they therefore cannot be accepted without challenge. There is a tendency to assuming that expressing these same theories in mathematical form creates absolute knowledge and eliminates this challenge."[135] Novick attributed the lack of challenge of mathematical models to the fear of humiliation. "Those of us who have only a limited training and a still more limited experience in mathematics are too often cowed by the symbols and are afraid to challenge them lest we be embarrassed by showing our ignorance."[136]

Many leading economists responded to Novick's critique, including Samuelson.[137] Admits Samuelson, "some mathematical research constitutes rather trivial economics no sensible person would deny."[138] And Samuelson also admits that simply learning more math won't solve the problem: "no matter how much mathematics you study, there is a frontier at which things become hard: by working with ever more general premises . . . you can succeed in making almost any problem hard."[139]

Yet, Samuelson is dismissive of the argument that the often-confusing nature of mathematics means that it should not be utilized. He perceives mathematics as a more efficient language through which to make logical arguments. As Samuelson argued in a paper published in 1952, "the problems of economic theory — such as the incidence of taxation, the effects of devaluation — are by their nature quantitative questions whose answers depend upon the superposition of many different pieces of quantitative and qualitative information. When we tackle them by words, we are solving the same equations as when we write up the equations."[140] And the choice of equations over words is simply due to the fact that math is more convenient. Samuelson argues that, "no sensible person who had at his command both the techniques of literary argumentation and mathematical manipulation would tackle by words alone a problem. . . . The convenience of mathematical symbolism for handling certain deductive inferences is, I think, indisputable."[141]

The controversy over the role of mathematics in economics continues today. And, for those who dislike the position of mathematics in economics, Samuelson is assigned a large proportion of the blame. Yet, it is clear that for economists today, math and economics are largely inseparable — possibly to a fault. As Alan Blinder of Princeton University puts it, "somewhere along the way, the warm embrace of mathematics developed first into an infatuation, and then into an obsession."[142] Indeed, the field of economics has developed to the point where one's math skills can determine the likelihood of one's future success as an economist — at a bare minimum, an individual lacking these skills is at a great disadvantage. Recent evidence suggests that a student's math skills can significantly influence the student's performance in introductory economics courses.[143] But as with almost any other issue in economics, there are others who disagree with these findings.[144] Whichever side one falls on in this debate, it is unquestionable that rigorous math skills are mandatory to complete a doctorate in economics today — and math skills are crucial for most areas of research, especially theory.

Samuelson discusses this very issue in a hypothetical conversation with a student. "I am interested in economic theory." Samuelson's student asks, "I know little mathematics. And when I look at the journals, I am greatly troubled. Must I give up hopes of being a theorist? Must I learn mathematics? If so, how much? I am already past twenty-one; am I past redemption?" Samuelson's answer: "Some of the most distinguished economic theorists, past and present, have been innocent of mathematics. Some of the most distinguished theorists have known some degree of mathematics. Obviously, you can become a great theorist without knowing mathematics. Yet it is fair to say that you will have to be that much more clever and brilliant."[145]

These words were published in 1952. Today, little economic theory is presented without mathematical treatment, and the probability of a young economist successfully publishing non-mathematical economic theory is very low. In this sense, Samuelson's approach to economic theory now dominates the field.

ALLEGIANCE TO THE FACTS

THE RESEARCH on which economists spend their lives toiling can be loosely classified as either "theoretical" or "empirical." Theoretical economic research strives to develop economic models that can be used to understand economic behavior. Empirical economic research tests the implications of theoretical models using statistical measurement of observable data. *Econometrics* is a branch of economics that studies the application of statistical methods to empirical economic research.

The models that economists develop are never perfect reflections of reality—reality is simply too complex to fully incorporate into an economic model. Instead, models represent an abstraction from reality. So what makes a theory a "good theory?" In the context of scientific theories, Stephen Hawking, the theoretical physicist writes, "A theory is a good theory if it satisfies two requirements: It must accurately describe a large class of observations on the basis of a model that contains only a few arbitrary elements. And it must make definite predictions about the results of future observations."[146] Now, economic theories are not pure scientific theories. Alan Blinder notes that "By the 1960s or 1970s, economics had been completely transformed into a technical discipline with all the trappings of science."[147] But economics is not *pure* science. This distinction is important, argues Frank Hahn. "Very many American economists regard economics as a 'science' and often refer to themselves as 'scientists.' This is not just a semantic matter. Behind these words there is a *Weltanschauung*, and that is the nineteenth-century view that what was achieved in the physical sciences can be achieved by the same means by the social sciences. This view, for all I know, may turn out to be correct. What is striking, however, is that so far economics has provided no evidence that it is."[148] Contrast this approach with the following quote from Milton Friedman: "In principle, I believe that economics has a scientific component no different in character from the scientific component of physics or chemistry or any of the other physical sciences. True, as those who believe otherwise often stress, the physicist can conduct controlled experiments and the economist cannot. But that is hardly sufficient grounds to deny the scientific character of economics."[149]

Samuelson, the master of the economic model, clearly agrees that regarding economics as a pure science is unwise. Warning us against "scientism," Samuelson observes, "I abhor the sins of scientism. I recognize that as social scientists, we can have relationships with the data we study that astronomers cannot have with the data they study."[150] After all, as scholars in a field that studies human economic behavior, economists effectively study themselves. Samuelson is also cognizant that alternative models can be used to describe a single set of data. Writes Samuelson, "Admittedly, a given field of data can be described in terms of alternative patterns of descriptions, particularly by disputing authorities who differ in the error tolerance they display towards different aspects of the data. Admittedly, observations are not merely seen or sensed but rather often are perceived in gestalt patterns that impose themselves on the data and even distort those data."[151]

Rachel McCulloch of Brandeis University tells of her experience with Samuelson:

> Paul Samuelson was my teacher in the Ph.D. micro course at MIT in spring 1967. The classes had a free-form quality that made them at the same time stimulating and frustrating. As a student new to the field of economics, I longed for a neat sum-mary of everything important to know, but that was definitely not what we were to receive! Each class would begin promisingly enough with a clear theme and maybe a couple of standard equations, but soon Paul would be off on a tangent, and then anything could happen. His lectures ranged widely over the history of economic theory and even the history of science. My notes for the class (which I still keep in my office) contain references to all the greats of economics from Adam Smith to Paul's own contemporaries, plus many anecdotes about eminent natural scientists going back to Newton and even earlier. Over the course of the term, we became familiar with many advances, but at least as many dead ends, in the progress of our discipline. In retrospect, Paul was helping us to understand the messiness of scientific research. Even the best thinkers had many strange notions and quirks of

personality. Or maybe that should be "especially the best thinkers"?

For Paul, the greatest of the great thinkers was Newton, and more than once he held forth on the reasons why Newton didn't publish sooner. (I'm not sure he actually said w*hat* Newton didn't publish sooner. The *Principia*? In fact Newton was curiously reluctant to publish anything—until faced with the risk that one of his contemporaries might get credit for the same results.) As I recall, there were four reasons. Of these, I and my friends from the class can remember three for sure: (1) Newton was introverted. (2) He wanted to recheck his calculations—Paul laughed merrily at the idea that any modern scientists would delay in order to do this. And (3) Newton did not want to acknowledge any debt to Hooke. But what was the fourth reason? This may have been his reluctance to acknowledge Leibniz's role in the invention of the calculus. If so, why do we all remember about rivalry with Hooke but not with Leibniz?

Looking back at my ancient lecture notes, there was something else different about the course. In the 1960s, MIT was remarkably Chicago-phobic, and rather mean-spirited jokes about Chicago economics and Chicago economists were common. But Paul gave free-market thinkers their due in his historical meanderings, and even made some favorable comments about Milton Friedman's contributions to microeconomics.[152]

While Samuelson is admittedly "primarily a theorist," he also stresses that "my first and last allegiance is to the facts."[153] Nonetheless, Samuelson's description of himself as "primarily a theorist" is quite accurate: Samuelson's academic output does not include empirical research. William Breit and Roger L. Ransom observe in their book *Academic Scribblers* that Samuelson "has always been highly skeptical of the ability of econometric models to predict future economic events."[154]

Samuelson admits his own early enthusiasm for econometrics and his subsequent disillusionment. "Let me make a confession. Back when I was 20 I could perceive the great progress that was being made in econometric *methods*. Even without foreseeing the onset of the computer age, with its cheapening of calculations, I expected that the new econometrics would enable us to narrow down the uncertainties of economic theories. We would be able to test and reject false theories. We would be able to infer new good theories. My confession is that this expectation has not worked out. . . . I never ignore econometric studies, but I have learned from sad experience to take them with large grains of salt."[155] The "sad experience" to which Samuelson refers may be his incorrect 1944 prediction in the *New Republic* that foretold of greater unemployment following the end of World War II, a prediction that subsequently was proven incorrect.[156] Samuelson describes this as a "large squared forecasting error on the downward side."[157] This mistake on Samuelson's part reminds us of the story of Nathan Milstein, the famous violinist, who was approached by an admirer and asked to play a false note, only to prove his humanity.

However, we must note that Samuelson is not a naïve falsificationist, that is, one who gives up on a paradigm or model when met with its first failure to predict. One bad prediction does not kill a model that is deeply grounded in reality. By making his paradigm more progressive via the dictates of reality, Samuelson also has a foot in the sophisticated falsificationist camp, that is, one who is ready to give up on a model when faced with frequent failures.[158]

Yet, Samuelson's skepticism toward econometrics does not take away from his belief that empirical relevance is crucial when developing theoretical models. "As you observe scientists and study the developments of disciplines," writes Samuelson, "when schools evolve and paradigms are born and die, it is forced upon you that *what ultimately shapes the verdicts of the scientist juries is an empirical reality out there.*"[159] Samuelson recognizes that mathematical models, no matter how aesthetically pleasing, are purposeless if they do not fit well with reality. While Samuelson, like all of us, dislikes being wrong, he describes himself as his own strongest critic and an eclectic economist, willing to consider multiple causations for an effect. "I am eclectic," writes Samuelson, "only because experience has shown that Mother Nature is eclectic."[160]

Samuelson's eclecticism extends beyond theoretical economics. János Kornai of Harvard University recalls the year 1989, just before the collapse of the Berlin wall, as follows:

By that time I had written the first book on the tasks of post-communist transition. It was published first in Hungarian, and soon there was also an

English edition under the title *The Road to a Free Economy*. Paul had already known me in person at that time. I was teaching at Harvard and living in Cambridge, and we met at various occasions. One day he called me and I was overwhelmed to learn that he had read my little book.[161]

Just few leading scholars were able to resist the temptation at that time to give self-assured advice to the transition countries. Paul was one of them. With utmost modesty he restricted himself to a few comments and questions.

At that time I was outraged by the unbearably high tax burden of Hungarians. I also thought that at a time when private business had just started to appear, fiscal policy must not weaken the profit incentive by a progressive income tax. Therefore I suggested a flat tax rate. Samuelson, a good American liberal, did not like my proposal and warned me that a flat tax rate could be quite unfair.

I was extremely happy to learn later that he had written a newspaper article which beside other topics commented on my book. It had a flattering title: *For Plan to Reform Socialism, Listen to János Kornai.* I quote the article: "I used to be asked by the Chinese how they should go about their transition toward a market economy. I would reply: Don't ask me, an expert on the mixed economy, how to reform a socialist state. Ask János Kornai of Budapest, who spends half his time as a Harvard professor . . . he will have a better feel for what the political traffic will bear."

And then the article continues this way: "Now I find that Dr. Kornai has written a brief book about the 'Economic Transition' [i.e. *The Road to a Free Economy*]. I have just seen its English translation and recommend it highly." The article gives a concise summary of the main ideas concerning free enterprise and the role of the state, approvingly. He included in the article the same warning he gave in our earlier conversation, namely that I go probably too far with the tax proposal hoping that I will have second thoughts on this matter later.

Let me mention one more point discussed in Samuelson's article. I was involved in a controversy at that time. Some influential American advisers to the former East-Bloc countries suggested a quick-fix solution to the ownership reform. I refused this proposal, and advocated a gradualist approach, supporting the organic development of a new middle-class. It was good to know that Paul is on my side. He explained to his readers my position in that matter, and then (I quote) wrote these lines: "The citizenry, Kornai insists, should develop 'social respect' toward the private sector. Envy and equating of profit-earners with crooks and sharks is counterproductive. Hungary is in need of *a new middle class*. Napoleon spoke slightingly of England as a nation of shopkeepers. Kornai is no Napoleon!"

These lines not only show Paul's deep understanding of the issue at stake, but demonstrate how wide his knowledge of history is. Nowadays a lot of economists tend to consider economic problems taken out of historical context, in some "timeless" fashion. Not Paul Samuelson! Not only does he *know* history (he would quote easily names of politicians or novelists of the Austrian-Hungarian empire of the late 19th century if he had a Hungarian sitting on his side at the dinner table), but he *understands the significance* of the history of a country precisely determining the feasibility or efficiency of certain policies and seeing clearly also the impossibility or the disadvantages of some other courses. This is a rare quality at a time when the education of economists has become excessively technical.[162]

Samuelson's grounding in "reality" can often be missed by students and critics, some of whom may perceive the avalanche of mathematical modeling that Samuelson has produced as evidence of unacceptable abstraction from reality. But while mathematics can indeed be misused to create imaginary castles in the sky, Samuelson uses math-ematical models for the exact opposite purpose: to create rigorous mathematical abstractions that are linked to reality and fact—facts that can be empirically verified or rejected. Samuelson's thorough demonstration of how mathematical modeling can improve our understanding of reality is argu-ably his most important contribution to economics.

ADDITIONAL NOTES AND SOURCES, CHAPTER 3

THE FOUR CHARACTERISTICS of mathematics that we describe
in order to justify the use of mathematics in economics are
loosely based on the introduction to Alpha C. Chiang's
Fundamental Methods of Mathematical Economics. For a
broader critique of mathematical modeling in economics,
of which there are plenty, we suggest E. Ray Canterbery's
The Making of Economics, particularly pages 199 through
202; Alan S. Blinder's "Economics Becomes a Science — or
Does it?"; and D.N. McCloskey's "Other Things Equal:
Samuelsonian Economics" in the *Eastern Economic Journal*;
among others. For an interesting discussion of the negative
effect that mathematics has on enrollment in economics
programs, see R. L. Bartlett's "Attracting 'Otherwise Bright
Students' to Economics 101" in the *American Economic
Review*.

Chapter 4: Samuelson the Celebrity

The common idea that success spoils people by
making them vain, egotistic, and self-complacent is
erroneous; on the contrary it makes them, for the
most part, humble, tolerant, and kind.
–W. Somerset Maugham

ECONOMISTS AND ACADEMICS in general do not have much difficulty appreciating Paul Samuelson's extraordinary contributions. Simply reading Samuelson's *Foundations of Economic Analysis* or browsing through the plethora of intellectual jewels displayed in the many volumes of *The Collected Scientific Papers of Paul A. Samuelson* makes these contributions evident. But one of the most compelling characteristics of Paul Samuelson is his ability to communicate equally well with all audiences, whether academics, students forced to take an economics class for the first time, or the wider public. If you limited your reading to Samuelson's academic writings, which are characterized by an unyielding theoretical rigor, you might get the impression that you were dealing with an alien of sorts—a creature simply too brilliant to communicate with the average human and whose ideas could only be understood by a few select academics.[163] Yet, Samuelson's true brilliance is his ability to flawlessly tune his writing to his audience, whether mathematically inclined economists and graduate students, introductory students reading his *Economics*, readers of his *Newsweek Magazine* column, or the government agencies and politicians he advised, including John F. Kennedy.[164] Indeed, one can argue that this is Samuelson's most important virtue.

Alan Brown tells us: "I consulted with him on various occasions, especially, since he was on the Advisory Board of the Committee on Comparative Urban Economics. He was willing to talk to me about the Committee originally because Abe Bergson, his very close friend and my former thesis advisor, was a member of the Committee, and it also helped that Tinbergen had conditionally agreed to be on the Board (the condition being that Samuelson would also agree to be on the Board). After Samuelson joined the Board, we were able to get some of the most helpful people: Kenneth Boulding, Evsey Domar, John Dunlop, Wassily Leontief, and Harvey Perloff (known as the 'father of urban economics' in the U.S.). Samuelson disclaimed any knowledge of the field of urban economics, but when I referred to an article in his collected papers, something he wrote twenty years before in urban economics, he became very animated: 'Oh, yes, I was invited by some architects to talk about economics and I tried to be intelligible.' It was a very clear article, and in spite of his disclaimer, he revealed more knowledge about urban economics than the specialists at the time."[165]

In this chapter, we will first take a closer look at Samuelson's famous textbook and the celebrity (and criticism) it attracted. We will then conclude with a look at "the spoils of battle" — some of the awards and honors Samuelson has received, including the Nobel Memorial Prize in Economics.

Economics 101

Samuelson's legendary textbook, straightforwardly titled *Economics*, most famously exemplifies Samuelson the writer. But how did *Economics* come to be written? Samuelson recalls how the head of the Department of Economics at MIT, Ralph Freeman, beseeched Samuelson to write an economics textbook. Freeman had a problem: MIT forced its juniors to take a compulsory course in economics. "They hate it," moaned Freeman, "We've tried everything. They still hate it."[166] And he made Samuelson an offer he couldn't refuse: "Paul, will you go on half time for a semester or two? Write a text the students will like. If they like it, yours will be good economics. Leave out whatever you like. Be as short as you wish. Whatever you come up with, that will be a vast improvement on where we are."[167] Samuelson accepted and took the task seriously. Three years later, "after night and summer slaving and following up on uncountable mimeograph handouts" the book was ready for publication.[168]

Samuelson published the first edition of the textbook with McGraw-Hill in 1948, though there was extensive interest from other publishers. Samuelson describes how two dozen publishers were "clamoring" for his text, yet he choose McGraw-Hill for the following reasons: "Reason 1: Macmillan and Prentice-Hall, the other giants back then, already had best-selling textbooks; McGraw-Hill did not. Reason 2: What clinched the deal was that McGraw-Hill had published the scholarly 2-volume treatise on *Business Cycles* by my Harvard teacher Joseph Schumpeter and had also published the 15-volume compendium on what had been learned at the MIT Radiation Laboratory where I had spent the War."[169] The original McGraw-Hill representative assigned to Paul Samuelson was an individual named Basil Dandison. Dandison had first met Samuelson at Harvard seven years earlier on December 8, 1941, having been introduced by the Harvard professor Seymour Harris.[170] The Dandison-Samuelson relationship was full of mutual admiration—in 1999, at the age of ninety-seven, Basil Dandison was still praising Samuelson: "It was a great thing for McGraw-Hill when Paul Samuelson decided to sign up with us." And to this Samuelson replied, "What a gentleman!"[171]

Now, the amiable relationship between Samuelson and McGraw-Hill should come as no surprise: *Economics* was a huge success. The first edition (1948) sold 121,453 copies and the second edition (1951) sold 137,256.[172] The high water mark was the sixth edition, which sold 441,941 copies. The eleventh edition (1980), the last that Samuelson wrote by himself, sold 196,185 copies; and sales remained strong for the twelfth (1985) and later editions, which were coauthored with William D. Nordhaus, a leading professor of economics at Yale University. The book is now in its seventeenth edition with a new version in the works.[173] In total, as of this writing, more than four million copies of *Economics* have sold, and it has been translated into forty-one languages. The book remains popular today, or as Nordhaus enthusiastically puts it, "The book is alive. Long live the book!"[174]

Interestingly, Samuelson never received an advance—an idea that most textbook authors would consider preposterous today. For example, Harvard economics professor Gregory

Mankiw, who was appointed as Chairman of the Council of Economic Advisors in 2003, received a $1.4 million advance in 1997 for his *Principles of Economics*, now in its third edition (SouthWestern, 2004). On his decision to accept lower royalties for international English-language editions, Samuelson explains, "My interest was not so much in dollars as in influencing minds."[175]

The huge success of *Economics* turned Samuelson into a celebrity. "A new layer of fame that I never dreamed of evolved," Samuelson reveals. "I was besieged by groupies reminiscent of Talmudic students crowding around famous rabbis. . . . The policeman at the door of the White House whispers, 'I am using your book at Georgetown night school.' The chap who sells me a newspaper at Harvard Square confides that at Northeastern he studied my book. . . . Wherever I go in Europe, Asia, or Latin America, strangers greet me as an old friend or old tormenter. I have never been to India, Russia, or China, but in my MIT office, I am asked to autograph copies of translations."[176]

The degree to which Samuelson's textbook has influenced students internationally should not be underestimated. Elhanan Helpman, the Israeli economist now at Harvard University, recalls how, as a young man, he discovered "a thick volume that was the Hebrew version of Samuelson's textbook. The translation was terrible. It employed convoluted Hebrew terms for simple economic concepts. Nevertheless, I fell in love with the book's content. What struck me most was the realization that one can in fact think systematically about complex social phenomena and describe them in precise language. All this was new to me, and my fascination grew with every page."[177]

János Kornai of Harvard University and Collegium Budapest, Hungary, explains that

Marxism-Leninism had a monopoly in the education of Hungarian economists in the 1950s. After the 1956 defeat of the Hungarian revolution I was determined to study proper contemporary economics on my own, teaching myself. I was twenty-eight years old at the time; not an inappropriate age for education. There were two books I got hold of. The first one was the last Hungarian economics textbook used at the university before the communist take-over, written by the distinguished Hungarian economist Farkas Heller. The other text was Samuelson's *Economics*. I'd heard about the book from a well-trained economist of the older generation, Professor Istvan Varga, who stood on the sidelines of the profession during the Stalinist period. I asked a friend who worked in foreign-trade and therefore had the possibility to travel to buy the book for me.

What a relief and intellectual pleasure it was to read these books, after being exposed for so many years exclusively to the Marxist doctrine! While I learnt a lot from the Heller book, I felt immediately the superiority of the Samuelson text. Not only because it was more up-to-date, but because of its didactic virtues, transparent organization, lucidity, examples and data convincingly illustrating the arguments—all the merits well appreciated by the millions of readers of this number one textbook. I cannot imagine a better introduction for a young person with the strong determination to become an economist.[178]

Economics grew into something more than just another obscure academic textbook; its wide popularity meant that it strongly influenced the way that economists, the American public, and the entire world perceived economics.[179] This also meant that Paul Samuelson faced both a tremendous amount of pressure to represent the ideas in the book and significant criticism by those who disagreed with his slant. Indeed, one cynical way of measuring the importance of a book is by observing the degree of criticism it receives. Interestingly, criticism of *Economics* began before the textbook was even published. Samuelson never forgot how a preliminary version of the textbook, distributed to his students before publication, faced a tremendous amount of opposition from some MIT alumni and board members — two groups that no academic can easily ignore.[180] One of these critics even listed 100 "heresies" in the text, and waved off Samuelson's attempts to respond, griping, "The whole tone is wrong. You do not inculcate sound economics. That is your trouble."[181] The same critic wanted the textbook vetted before publication. Eventually, the president of MIT at the time, Karl Compton, stepped in and threatened to resign if Samuelson was censored. He was successful, and *Economics* was released to the world.

As *Economics* grew increasingly popular, the criticism amplified, both from the right and the left.[182] Samuelson remarks, "In one lifetime, while adhering to the same eclectic liberalism, I have been at first denounced as avant garde and later castigated as a running jackal of capitalism."[183]

But Samuelson understands the game. In the introduction to the fifteenth edition of *Economics*, Samuelson writes, "People differ about economic policies. Tempers flare out, arguments are shrill, and different schools and ideologies grow up—each convinced that its view of the simple truth is the one-and-only correct version. After a lifetime in the trenches, my advice to beginning students when you contemplate any such hot debate is this: Hang on to your wallet. Economic laws are truly complicated."[184]

  One fascinating example of the kind of criticism Samuelson received is the 1977, two-volume book *Anti-Samuelson*, written by Marc Linder, who is currently a professor of law at the University of Iowa. *Anti-Samuelson* represented "an attempt to follow S in his presentation of bourgeois theory." "S," or course, refers to Samuelson; and the criticism is from the left wing of ideological thought, and clearly heartfelt—it is a very long book. The book is organized in direct relation to specific chapters of Samuelson's text. The following is characteristic of the criticism: "His attention is focused on the 'problems' of the present and their possible solution *within* capitalism. This is S's unspoken value judgment: as a practical man, a 'citizen,' he supports capitalism and opposes socialism. Accordingly, he tries to foist these values on his reader. That, of course, is his prerogative, but it would be nice if he would at least warn the unwary reader. However, matters change when he disseminates these views in the guise of scientist. . . . But S's theory is not simply demagoguery. By far the more significant aspect of the ideological role of bourgeois economic theory is its unconscious refusal to recognize the possibility of the existence of problems serious enough to cause the demise of the capitalist mode of production."[185] As active participants in a capitalist society, it is dangerously easy for us to discard this criticism as radical. Yet, it is also true that Samuelson's coverage of Marx and socialism has evolved over time, and it is no wonder that leftists experienced a sense of abandonment. Mark Skousen observes, "References to Marx and international socialism are scarce and random in the early editions. In the first edition, Marx was declared 'quite wrong' in his prediction that the 'poor are becoming poorer'. . . . Attacks on Marxism expanded with each edition. . . . But starting with the ninth edition, references to the ideas and followers of Karl Marx and Friedrich Engels expanded dramatically. . . . However, this expanded coverage did not mute his criticism of Marxist beliefs. With the fall of the Soviet Union, the discussion of Marx shrank from 12 pages in the fourteenth edition to three pages in the fifteenth (1995) edition."[186]

Samuelson was also criticized heavily from the right. Consider Mark Skousen, an economist and descendant of Benjamin Franklin, whose extensive review of the evolving nature of *Economics* was published in a 1997 article in the *Journal of Economic Perspectives*.[187] According to Skousen, "In reading Samuelson's earlier editions, a student might reasonably conclude that there are no other schools of thought, at least in the mainstream. In fact, of course, Keynesian thought was the subject of furious debate in economics departments across the country through the 1940s and into the 1950s, as young economists steeped in Keynesian thinking entered professorial jobs and collided with the old guard. In the late 1950s and 1960s, as economists explored how certain modeling structures could

express either Keynesian or monetarist insights, it was fair
to claim broad acceptance of the 'neo-classical synthesis'
as a modeling strategy."[188]

And in an article in *Forbes Magazine*, Skousen continued the attack: "Samuelson spent whole chapters in serious
discussion of the socialist economics of the Soviet Union
and China, while writing little or nothing on the success
stories of West Germany, Japan, the East Asian Tigers or
Chile. . . . He had numerous sections on 'market failure,'
while offering little on 'government failure.' He criticized
laissez-faire, favored progressive taxation and endorsed the
pay as you go Social Security program."[189]

Samuelson does indeed take clear positions on the ideological battles, and some of his positions he later modifies.
One position that has been attacked repeatedly by the right
was Samuelson's evaluation of the Soviet economy. The following quote, from the thirteenth edition of *Economics*, is
perceived as particularly bothersome: "The Soviet economy
is proof that, contrary to what many skeptics had earlier
believed, the socialist command economy can function and
even thrive."[190] As even Skousen will admit, "Samuelson is
willing to change his mind when the facts demand it."[191]
While Samuelson remains proud of the early editions, he
recognizes that, in hindsight, he could have made some
changes. Rereading the 1948 edition fifty years after publication, Samuelson was quite impressed. "To my surprise,
it read much better than I could ever have suspected. No
wonder it was an instant best-seller, which set a new pattern
for all the late twentieth century economic textbooks."[192]
Yet, he was also self critical, admitting that he had to "wince
at various nonoptimalities that are obvious from hindsight.

Fiscal policy was given too much emphasis at the expense of monetary policy. Yes. Can this be excused by the fact that not until the 1951 Accord did the Federal Reserve get back its freedom to exercise an autonomous monetary policy? Admittedly, that is an excuse in part. But is it not a duty for the economics writer to pound on the table and nag against bad institutional policies?"[193]

What critics fail to recognize, Samuelson argues, is the era in which the early editions of the textbook were written. The key question to ask is not whether the text overemphasized one stream of thought over another. After all, Samuelson reminds us, Milton Friedman's early writing never incorporated his own later work! Instead, the question that Samuelson poses is, "Was the Samuelson elementary text lagging behind the plethora of emerging intermediate macroeconomic textbooks in the 1948–1985 era or a pioneering engine in evolutionary progress?"[194] As an inexact science, economic thought evolves in response to new developments—perception of reality today may well appear as unrealistic tomorrow. "Funeral by funeral," argues Samuelson, "economics does make progress. Darwinian impact of reality melts away even the prettiest of fanciful theories and the hottest of ideological frenzies. But there are fits and starts along the way."[195] More simply, Samuelson summarizes this philosophy as "Be wrong, but don't stay wrong."[196]

Why was Samuelson's *Economics* so successful? There was, after all, significant competition, such as *Principles of Economics* by Frederic Garver and Alvin Hansen; *Economic Principles, Problems and Policies* by William Kiekhoffer; *Modern Economic Society* by Sumner Slichter; and *Elementary*

Economics by Fred Fairchild, Edgar Furniss, and Norman Buck; among others.[197] Samuelson attributes the success of *Economics* to "book content," noting that competing texts failed to address the compelling problems of the day. "When 5,000 banks failed and mortgage delinquencies were in the millions, the bestselling texts limned the certainties of Say's Law!"[198] And many consider the coverage Samuelson gave to the Keynesian revolution as *Economics'* most important characteristic. But Robert Solow of MIT disagrees, arguing that "the introduction of Keynesian ideas was not the major innovation. Paul's was probably the first truly postwar textbook, in the sense that it represented economics as it was in the postwar period and as it became, largely because of Paul's other career as a writer of economics for economists."[199]

Indeed, the success of *Economics* likely flowed from a combination of these factors. And the fact that Samuelson was a leading economist with a reputation as a *wunderkind* must have also influenced professors to assign *Economics* to their students. But what is undeniable, regardless of one's ideological perspective, is that *Economics* is wonderfully written. As the economist Stanley Fischer, President of Citigroup International and Governor of Israel's Central Bank, puts it: "To read *Economics* is to have a glimpse of the extraordinary mind that created it: undogmatic, generous to predecessors and contemporaries, encyclopedic, of course brilliant, and, most remarkably, skeptical, not inclined to take itself too seriously. Those are not properties that come in that combination very often, least of all in a textbook."[200] And from this, we all continue to benefit.

The Spoils of Battle

SAMUELSON'S INTELLECTUAL CONTRIBUTIONS are many, beginning in his days as a student at the University of Chicago and Harvard University, and continuing throughout his career at MIT until the present. His written contributions—characterized by their sheer volume and mathematical rigor—are of continuing relevance today. In return, the world expressed its appreciation through remuneration in the form of a flurry of honors and awards, not to mention healthy book sales. Simply put, Samuelson has received almost every important honor and award that an economist could possibly receive. Among his many achievements, Samuelson received the American Economic Association's first John Bates Clark Award in 1947, which is awarded to the living economist under the age of forty that is judged to have "made the most distinguished contribution to the main body of economic thought and knowledge." Samuelson also received the Albert Einstein Medal in 1970 and the National Medal of Science in 1996. He was President of the Econometrics Society (1953), the American Economic Association (1961), and the International Economic Association (1965). "As yet," jokes Samuelson, "there is no Galaxy Political Economy Club."[201] He was a Guggenheim Fellow (1948–1949) and a Ford Foundation Research Fellow (1958–1959). He has received honorary degrees from many universities. Writes Samuelson, "Peer recognition came early and often. . . . Just as it is the first million that is the hardest, one honor leads to another. After the first dozen honorary degrees, all it takes is longevity to double the number."[202]

Samuelson most appreciates the honorary degrees from the institutions where he completed his education. Referring to himself by his initials, PAS, Samuelson writes "The first such degree — from Chicago, alma mater and basilica of a church he no longer believed in — PAS found most touching. When Harvard honored a prophet in his own country, he also liked that."[203] In addition to his honorary degrees, MIT established the Paul A. Samuelson Professorship in Economics in 1991 in his honor.

But of course most prominent of all is Samuelson's receipt of the Nobel Memorial Prize in Economics in 1970. At the time, the Nobel Memorial Prize in Economics was a new development, having been established by the Bank of Sweden (Sveriges Riksbank) in 1968 to celebrate its 300th anniversary. In its first year, the Nobel Memorial Prize in Economics was jointly awarded to Ragnar Frisch of Norway and Jan Tinbergen of the Netherlands. Samuelson received his award the following year, making him the first American to receive it. Assar Lindbeck, the University of Stockholm Economics Professor and former Chairman of the prize committee for the Nobel Memorial Prize in Economics, defined Samuelson's work as dealing "largely with the analytical structures of theoretical economic models, often highlighting the formal similarity of these structures, and clarifying the conditions for consistency, equilibrium, stability and efficiency of the economic system."[204] This categorization is unsurprising given Samuelson's emphasis on theoretical modeling. More interestingly, as Linbeck notes, Samuelson's prize citation is not very specific when detailing his contributions, simply indicating that Samuelson raised "the level of analysis in economic sciences."

Winning a Nobel is a good thing; we don't have to convince you of that. And Paul Samuelson enjoyed receiving the award. "Few things in life bring undiluted pleasure, but this one actually did." But surely Samuelson wasn't too surprised to hear he had won the prize; after all, Samuelson's contributions were widely celebrated, and as the awards and honors piled up, Samuelson certainly recognized a trend. Indeed, for its first decade, the Nobel Memorial Prize committee had to deal with a "heavy backlog of rather obvious candidates."[205] Yet, Samuelson asserts, "The honor was a pleasant surprise and came early, but not so early to worry even me."[206] The "pleasant surprise," to which Samuelson refers is likely due to the fact that many of his contributions followed, chronologically, the important contributions of others. The fact that Samuelson was one of the first to receive the prize is therefore indicative of the level at which the Nobel Memorial Prize committee valued his contributions.

One side benefit of receiving a Nobel is that it definitely doesn't hurt one's self-esteem. Samuelson explains why this is important. "I long ago enunciated the doctrine that scholars work for their self-esteem, in the sense of what they all agree to judge meritorious. However, once your need for glory in the eyes of others has been somewhat appeased, you become free to work for your own approval. The job you think well done is the one that brings true bliss."[207] And to Samuelson, satisfaction with one's own work is the true goal; as the winner of the 1986 Nobel Memorial Prize in economics, James Buchanan, recalls, "when my Nobel award was announced in 1986, I got a nice note from Samuelson congratulating me, and with an ending line that I recall with pleasure. He said something like 'and best of all, you got it your way.' "[208]

Does the celebrity matter to Samuelson? Certainly he doesn't mind it much, or try to hide from it. But the recognition for which Samuelson strove is that which flows from contributions to economic science. "No celebrity as a *Newsweek* columnist," Samuelson insists, "no millions of clever-begotten speculative gains, no power as the Svengali or Rasputin to the prince and president could count as a pennyweight in my balance of worth against the prospect of recognition for having contributed to the empire of science."[209] Because there is this tension between striving for perfection and never truly reaching it, no scientist or artist is ever satisfied. We owe to Martha Graham the following central insight on the subject: "There is no satisfaction whatever at any time. There is only a queer, divine dissatisfaction; a blessed unrest that keeps us marching and makes us more alive than the others."

ADDITIONAL NOTES AND SOURCES, CHAPTER 4

THIS CHAPTER PROVIDES a brief overview of some of the issues surrounding *Economics,* as well as an overview of some of Samuelson's more notable awards and honors. For those who did not have to buy the textbook as a student, may we recommend that you find a way to purchase or borrow a copy—it's a remarkably easy to read and engaging textbook, and we are sure you will quickly agree that its popularity is not coincidental. You may also wish to visit McGraw-Hill's Samuelson webpage, at www.mhhe.com/economics/samuelson, which include the insightful preface and other free material from the textbook. As of this writing, the latest edition available is the seventeenth, though another edition will appear shortly. For those interested in Marc Linder, author of *Anti-Samuelson,* visit his webpages at www.law.uiowa.edu/faculty/marc-linder.php. For those interested in Mark Skousen, the individual whose criticism-from-the-right of Samuelson we featured, visit his webpages at www.mskousen.com. Regarding the Nobel Memorial Prize in Economics, the Nobel Foundation provides a plethora of information, at www.nobel.se/economics.

Chapter 5: Samuelson the Teacher:

Two Personal Recollections

IN THE PROCESS of writing this book, we were honored to have received correspondences from a number of leading economists in which they relate their personal recollections of Paul A. Samuelson as colleague and teacher. In this section, we include the full correspondence from Avinash Dixit of Princeton University and Lawrence R. Klein of the University of Pennsylvania, winner of the 1980 Nobel Prize.

AVINASH DIXIT:
PAUL SAMUELSON AS TEACHER

MY MOST VIVID memories of Paul Samuelson come from two of his courses I took as a graduate student at MIT in 1966–67. The awe in which we students regarded him was doubled in this setting, because he usually taught at 9 a.m., when he was wide awake and we were still half asleep. He would write his handouts at the last minute on blue spirit duplication masters, run off copies himself in the department's machine room, and bring them to class. This gave his classes the freshness and spontaneity that are so sorely missing nowadays, when most lecturers and seminar speakers bring carefully prepared and slick overhead transparencies and Power-Point presentations, and mostly just read from them.

How good was his teaching? That depended on how well-prepared you were. His lecture style was not the best if you needed to learn the basics. But if you had done your advance reading, and knew most of the basics, he was brilliant. He showed you the subtleties and nuances of the subject, gave an account of how modern economic theory came into being—after all, he had created so much of it and had been present at the creation of the rest—and most importantly, conveyed a way of thinking about economics that would last you a lifetime. In short, you learned all the methods and skills for research that the cut-and-dried world of the textbooks left out.

As memorable as his research insights were his anecdotes about economists. Adam Smith, Ricardo, Marshall, Edgeworth, Keynes, Schumpeter, Irving Fisher, and above all Frank Ramsey, came alive for us in a way that taught us to respect the history of the subject and to appreciate the height of the shoulders of these giants, while at the same time making us smile at their human foibles. Irving Fisher's touching faith in the permanence of stock market valuations at the height of the 1920s bubble was matched by Joan Robinson's equally touching faith in everything Chairman Mao told her about the Chinese economy. Speaking of Joan Robinson, who can forget Paul's caricature of her visit to the United States: "She was taken in a sealed train from coast to coast—from Paul Baran to Paul Sweezy" (both of these are Marxists).

And there was Frank Ramsey, on his first day as an undergraduate at Cambridge, wanting to discuss with Ogden (his philosophy tutor) some ideas he had about essence and being. After listening, Ogden said, "These notions are rather like those of Kant." "Kant? Who is he?" was Ramsey's reply. "Immanuel Kant was the author of this book I'll lend you, *Kritik der reinen Vernunft*." "But it's in German, sir, and I don't know any German." "That's all right, I'll lend you this dictionary." A couple of weeks later Ramsey came back to Ogden saying "Kant has it almost right, but . . ." Paul took special and visible delight in telling this story, clearly recognizing in Ramsey a kindred spirit in precocity and genius.

What is the single most important thing I learned from Paul, and have tried to use throughout my research career? It is a sense of unity of the subject—of economics, and of the mathematical methods used in economic analysis. I learned to view all the "fields" into which economics is conventionally divided as intricately linked pieces of one big puzzle, with a common framework of concepts and methods of analysis—choice, equilibrium, and dynamics.

As for the role of mathematics, nothing explains it better than an anecdote Paul told us about J. Willard Gibbs, the famous mathematical physicist. Gibbs was renowned for never saying a word at Yale faculty meetings. But once when the faculty was discussing a proposal to let students choose either a foreign language or mathematics, Gibbs interjected, "Mathematics is a language." Paul improved this to "Mathematics is language." Viewed thus, it should be a tool for thinking as well as for communication. The dichotomy that many of us make between "economics" or "intuition" on the one hand and "mathematics" on the other is just as artificial as that between fields like international trade and industrial organization. Ideally, mathematics and intuition should fuse into one's overall Weltanschauung about economics. And incidentally, such sprinkling of words from other languages — to lighten the main discourse that was phrased in the logical and precise but dry language of mathematics, perhaps — was another trait many of us picked up from Paul.

Paul Samuelson showed us, through his own research and teaching, how uniquely well suited mathematical language is for studying economics, where many entities are interconnected by mutual linkages of cause and effect, and randomness has a big role. Probably more than anyone else in the twentieth century, he transformed the way economists think and write.

Lawrence R. Klein:
Vignettes of the Young Paul Samuelson

THE MASSACHUSETTS INSTITUTE OF TECHNOLOGY (MIT) had a long tradition, rooted in the latter part of the nineteenth century, of providing economics education to undergraduate students in science and engineering, not surprisingly related to the joint interests and activities of Francis A. Walker (president of MIT and of the American Economic Association). The Institute, nevertheless, was not noted for its teaching and research in economics. Undergraduate economics education was regarded as a "service" activity. At a more advanced level, there was some teaching and research in industrial engineering, but this was not the basis of MIT's fame in economics.

With an underlying theme of technological progress, MIT initiated a graduate economics doctoral program in the academic year 1941–42. The earliest entering classes were small — approximately ten admissions — well financed by scholarships and attractive to doctoral candidates by the outstanding presence of one person, Paul A Samuelson. I do not plan to dwell on the issue of why Harvard did not offer an immediate position to its most distinguished Ph.D. candidate in 1941, but Harvard's monumental loss and MIT's corresponding gain shaped the development of America and, indeed, world economics for the whole of the remaining decades of the twentieth century — and many more decades to come. I was not in the first entering Ph.D. group of 1941–42, but came fresh from the University of California/Berkeley, in September 1942. Among the *vignettes* of this note, I do not propose to focus on my own appraisal, but to describe what student life under the influence of Paul Samuelson during those early days of MIT economics was like.

American economics, at the time, 1941, was fully occupied with analysis of a wartime build-up following the Great Depression and interpretation of John Maynard Keynes' *General Theory of Employment, Interest, and Money*. This is important because Paul Samuelson's period of writing *The Foundations of Economic Analysis* as a Junior Fellow at Harvard (just down the road — Massachusetts Avenue — from MIT), where he had very close contact in economic discussions with leading expositors and interpreters of Keynes among students and faculty at Harvard.

He made it known to us (the early doctoral aspirants at MIT) that we had to breathe, live, sleep, and wrestle with the intricate new developments in economic thinking that absorbed the attention of the Harvard group, from which he had just shifted locale. But he did not really shift.

He lived a stone's throw from Harvard Yard and sent us, from MIT, to seminars at Harvard, especially by visiting notables in economics and to regular lectures by leading Harvard professors (Hansen, Schumpeter, Leontief, and especially E.B. Wilson who was instrumental in his coming to MIT and who gave us magnificent lectures about Keynes, Tinbergen, Gibbsian thermodynamics and his own versions of neoclassical economics).

At MIT, Paul Samuelson's lectures on microeconomics and macroeconomics formed the centerpieces of our education, covering both theory and policy. He taught us in many different ways. We students used to compete with one another to see who could spend the most minutes in one-on-one discussion with him. Such meetings were not entirely devoted to issues of his graduate-level lectures, but also to the development of more satisfactory reading materials for the service courses that we students had to teach, especially to large classes of naval trainees. Paul effectively re-wrote the materials for MIT's service teaching in economics. They came as preliminary chapters for his next big triumph, *Economics: An Introductory Analysis*, which were smoothed and perfected into the world's most popular economics textbook (principles) of the day. About Keynesian economics: he remarked that once it found its way into beginning textbooks, its future was assured. He did just that, starting with Keynesian ideas in early mimeographed segments.

Paul conducted his advanced classes in a particular style. He called upon unsuspecting students to answer tricky questions about economic behavior that required fast thinking, immediately. He took votes on yes-or-no interpretations of definite statements and succeeded in embarrassing us in front of the whole class. It became a case of trying to guess who would be called upon for the coming day and what the questions would be. We all tried, in vain, to outguess him and avoid being at a loss for words in class.

The same techniques that he used in graduate classes were displayed with even greater impact, when senior economists, from the world over, came to Harvard for lectures. I remember, in particular, that Abba Lerner dropped by, after an artistic visit to Provincetown on Cape Cod and had to say, eventually, to a packed audience at Littauer Center that "I admit that Mr. Samuelson is right" about *the* supply-demand imbalance that determines *the* interest rate. It was often said by younger economists that some of the more senior faculty members at Harvard were unsympathetic toward his appointment because he had publicly embarrassed them in much the same manner that he won the argument with Abba Lerner. Although Paul Samuelson's ties with Harvard economics are much better known, his early training and interest in the subject occurred at the University of Chicago. One day, Gale Johnson stopped by my room at the Cowles Commission (after I relocated from MIT) to say that Paul was coming to visit Chicago and be interviewed about an appointment there in the late 1940s. Gale declared, on the spot, that the joint faculty membership of Milton Friedman and Paul Samuelson would bring immediate and clear superiority to Chicago. I mentioned this to Trygve Haavelmo who knew Paul from his (Trygve's) prior extended visit to Cambridge, MA. Trygve said instantaneously that we must see if Paul would be available for dinner, at the end of a day's visit.

At the end of the day, we met (Paul, Trygve, and me) at a restaurant near the Chicago campus and immediately questioned Paul about the tone of his interview meetings during the day. "What kind of questions did they ask?" Paul responded that they wanted to know about the readings that he used for the basic theory classes. He responded that he taught Alfred Marshall's *Principles* and had the class reading from that book. In amazement, that line of questioning by the Chicagoans promptly ceased.

A chance encounter had occurred a few days earlier. I met, entering the Social Science Building, walking from the Bookstore, W. Allen Wallis and Jacob Marschak in close intensive conversation. Inside the entrance Marschak stopped me and said to Wallis that I would have an answer to their conversational question: Who is the world's greatest living economist? I promptly responded, without hesitation, that the appropriate answer was Paul Samuelson. Marschak said that he agreed with that, but Allen Wallis said that it was Milton Friedman. I protested and went on to explain why Samuelson was my choice, without any doubt.

As I met economists with diverse affiliations, at many general meetings, the first thing that they mentioned to me on learning that I came to Chicago (the Cowles Commission) straight from Ph.D. training at MIT was "What is Paul Samuelson up to now?" Any economist worth his salt at that time was touched, in one way or another, by the young Paul Samuelson whose professional fame was familiar everywhere, even before the publication of *Economics*.

Two illustrious scholars in econometrics and mathematical economics appeared frequently in Chicago, John von

Neumann, between trains, on his way to and from Los Alamos, and Abraham Wald, to discuss the interesting developments in econometrics, taking place at the Cowles Commission. Independently, at dinnertime conversation at the Quadrangle Club, both remarked in open praise about the intellectual achievements of Paul Samuelson.

Wherever my academic and professional paths took me over the next few years — Oslo, Stockholm, Copenhagen, the Hague, Paris, Cambridge, Oxford — the same queries about Paul Samuelson's latest achievements, especially with the textbook, *Economics: An Introductory Analysis* after 1948 and reactions to his style of teaching and discourse, which made such an impression on me during student days at MIT, but were not appreciated in some European centers. In spite of concern about being embarrassingly trapped in public debate there was remarkable appreciation about one thing, especially in Cambridge, England; namely that Paul knew so much about discussion-group interchange in the course of trying to understand fully Keynes' *General Theory* that his personal analyses of what Joan Robinson, Austin Robinson, Richard Kahn, Piero Sraffa, James Meade and other members of the informal group said were as accurate as if he had been present.

One way or another, I have served on committees or symposia, or discussion groups with Paul Samuelson, over more than seven decades, and note an interesting softening of position, certainly in the way one's personality comes across. I cannot say exactly when this softening began, but I first detected it in the 1950s, a couple of years after Paul's first trip abroad in 1948, following the enthusiastic reception of *Economics*.

Some seminar notes on Lectures in Econometrics that were discovered by the editor of *Statistical Science* (1991, 320–330) are noteworthy. Joseph Ullman and I took these seminar notes from 1942–43, as Paul's students who organized these meetings. He wrote a background piece for their re-printing in published form, and this reveals a soft and deep interpretation of the many distinguished participants, especially from the point of view of their bringing old world European views to the great enhancement of our educational system in the realm of American academia.

Conclusion

WHO IS Paul Samuelson? In this book, we have met Samuelson the student, the mentor, the policy maker, the philosopher, the theorist, and the celebrity. However, Paul Samuelson is more than the sum of all of these parts: The very words "Paul Samuelson" represent a veritable brand name for an approach to economics that is characterized by brilliance, rigor, and, most of all, confidence. Samuelson aggressively communicates bold positions to a huge audience and, at the same time, is saved from hubris by a self-depreciating and razor-sharp wit. Yet, Samuelson's voice is that of a confidant, carefully revealing secrets—and welcoming the reader closer to the warm campfire of those "in the know." And this is no facade; Samuelson is renowned for his personal warmth and caring. But it is also inescapable that a vast gulf separates us from Samuelson; any economist can only be awed at the magnificence of his contributions. For while Samuelson tells us that he perceives himself as having "an important role in the symphony orchestra."[210] We argue that his role was that of the conductor for the economists of the second half of the twentieth century.

Today, we live in deeply troubling times, as terrorists pursue agendas with apparently unlimited depravity and nihilism, and the fabric of our society is tested by acrimonious debates regarding appropriate responses. We can take comfort in the fact that twentieth century economists such as Paul Samuelson were able to achieve and excel while their world was in turmoil—for if they were able to achieve their contributions under such conditions, there is hope for the current and future generations.

In closing, we hope that you found this book interesting and insightful, and we hope we've done at least partial justice to our subject, Paul A. Samuelson. For those new to economics, we also hope that this book will encourage you to embark on further intellectual explorations into the world of economic thought. Samuelson, characteristically, puts it best: "Always it is better to travel than to arrive."[211] Our final wish to our readers is, therefore, *bon voyage!*

Appendix 1:

A Selection of Samuelson's Wise Sayings[212]

"In economics it takes a theory to kill a theory; facts can only dent the theorist's hide (2, 1568)."

"The science of economics does not provide simple answers to complex social problems (2, 1325)."

"A good economist has good judgment about economic reality (3, 775)."

"How a man uses a concept often throws light on what he thinks he means by it (?, 1607)."

"We must get the best guidance possible from experience itself (2, 1376)."

"There are no rules concerning the proper role of government that can be established by a priori reasoning (2, 1423)."

"Efficiency is hard to define, even harder to measure, and still harder to improve. It is easy to talk idly about efficiency (2, 1706)."

"The very name of my subject, economics, suggests economizing or maximizing (3, 2)."

"Nature is a great Economist, or economizer. Nature acts as if she has a purpose and aims (3, 455)."

"Today when we defend the rights of property, we often do so in the name of the individual rights of those who own property or hope one day to do so. The tides of modern politics pay little regard to the older view that property in all its prerequisites is a natural right (3, 630)."

"Individual human liberties have an ethical primacy over freedom associated with property and commercial activity . . . human rights are to be accorded ethical primacy over property rights (3, 632)."

"There is no ironclad presumption that profit seeking laissez-faire will lead to the social optimum (4, 147)."

"Advocates of freer trade—and I consider myself in this class—must not overstate their case. Protection can help special groups; it can even help special large groups (2, 861)."

"Under Darwinian competition . . . labor as much hires capital goods and land as capital hires labor and land (3, 27)."

"It is better to be left with an empty mind than with one filled with nonsense — with deductive inconsistencies and fanciful empirical hypotheses (4, 119)."

"As so often happens in the history of thought, the greater name drives out the lesser one (3, 678)."

"Each new theorem, each new insight, is like money in the bank, waiting to be drawn upon in some quite unexpected connection (3, 687)."

"He who goes out each morning to invent the wheel furthers his vanity more than his locomotion (3, 688)."

"We must warn in the strongest terms against confusing the conditions of real life with those of the scores of analytical articles in the financial journals (4, 528)."

"Even a stopped clock is periodically right, but at times that only those with a good watch can identify (5, 276)."

"The history of science shows that being an important influence in politics is not a way of holding lasting fame in the annals of scholarship (5, 279)."

"It is better to have a theory with imperfect foundation that gives some fit to the fact than to have an impeccable theory that doesn't at all fit the facts (5, 290)."

"If it does not pay to do an act once, it will not pay to do it twice, thrice . . . or at all (5, 554)."

"I also harbor a Hippocratic Oath: an economist, other things equal, should do no harm; in formulating the odds and stating the main reasons behind them, he should come clean on the uncertainties (5, 562)."

"To know our country we must have traveled abroad (3, 692)."

"Above all, the chief property of money is its vulgarity, as is illustrated by many an aphorism of folk wisdom. You can see what the Almighty thinks of money when you look at the people he gave it to. Money has no pride and no shame, it's not particular who it goes to (3, 6980)."

"The simplest things are often the most complicated to understand fully (4, 3)."

"The man in the street will not believe the assertion that high-paid American workers can compete with imported goods made by low paid foreign workers (4, 584)."

"It is death to rationality to disregard evidence and experience (4, 795)."

"You know that a theorem has really arrived and even gone by its full bloom when the literature begins to add rebuttals and qualifications to it (4, 847)."

"Never underestimate the blinding power of a beautiful mistake (5, 397)."

"Science, even inexact science is public knowledge, reproducible for analysis by everyone (5, 564)."

"To live is to change one's mind (5, 890)."

"The human mind thinks in terms of overdramatic case-studies (5, 892)."

"The economists I know are, by and large, not demonstrably better at spending or saving their money than other people; nor at outguessing the stock market (2, 1624)."

"With the assistance of mathematics, I can see a property of the ninety-nine dimensional surface hidden from the naked eye (3, 7)."

"By examining the sick we learn something about those who are well; and by examining those who are well we may also learn something about the sick (3, 13)."

"Easy communication can add to knowledge; it can also add to deadweight loss! (3, 33)."

"An automatic computer can forecast better than an official government agency. But an analyst with judgment can do better than an automatic computer (4, 831)."

"There is content in Smith's doctrine of the Invisible Hand. It tells us an important half-truth. A half-truth is a half-falsehood . . . Competitive equilibrium does not represent the best state of the world (4, 863–4)."

"The art of political economy is to know when and how to modify abstract models to take account of the discrepancies between them and the real world (5, 915)."

"Markets will not regulate themselves; government rules of the road are necessary (5, 925)."

"The scientist, as with the housewife, finds his work is really never done (3, 3)."

"An analogy to the problem of stability and planning is provided by a bicycle. A bicycle is highly unstable: unless set just right (and reset just right if perturbed), it will fall cumulatively away from equilibrium (3, 251)."

"Clearly I was ripe to accept, a few years later, Keynes' proposal that money wage rates be accepted as if they were 'sticky.' This was not a perfect bicycle, but it was the best wheel in town (5, 285)."

"Classical economists have always emphasized that channeling resources away from current consumption and toward capital formation is an important way of increasing the ability of an economic system to produce more in the future (2, 1400)."

"Libertarians fail to realize that the price system is, and ought to be, a method of coercion. Nature is not so bountiful as to give each of us all the goods he desires. We have to be coerced out of such a situation, by the nature of things (2, 1415)."

"Economists cannot forecast well . . . but experience shows that they forecast the economy better than any other group thus far discovered (2, 1674)."

"It cannot be restated too often that mastery of mathematics textbooks is neither a necessary nor sufficient condition for mastery of economics (2, 1652)."

"Common-sense economics may indeed be all that anyone must use in the end. But it takes the most uncommon sense and wisdom to know just which part of the filing case of muddled notions that men call common sense is relevant to a particular problem.

Common sense, and folklore generally, lack empirical content (2, 1667)."

"Know thy enemy is good advice for anyone, for to understand the full implications of a theory is to begin to understand its limitations (3, 220)."

"In principle, full employment with reasonable price stability could be attained by an appropriate fiscal policy (3, 590)."

"A mixed economy in a society where people are by custom tolerant of differences in opinion, may provide greater personal freedom and security of expression than does a purer price economy where people are less tolerant (3, 628)."

"Traffic lights coerce me and limit my freedom. Yet in the midst of a traffic jam on the unopened road, was I really 'free' before there were lights? . . . When we introduced the traffic light, we have, although the arch individualist may not like the new order, by cooperation and coercion created for ourselves greater freedom (3, 629)."

"Growth is no end by itself, but without growth modern problems are unlikely to get solved (3, 709)."

"To be a great scientist, you don't have to produce shelves of books. You just have to produce at least one great idea (5, 273)."

Appendix 2:

What It Means to Be an Economist

- Economists come to logical solutions through inferences and abstraction.

- Economists look for answers to day-to-day problems, incorporating other disciplines such as history, politics, education, and sociology.

- Economists consider opportunity cost, which includes tradeoffs, or the cost of one thing in terms of another. Since scarcity prevails, anything we do necessitates foregoing something else.

- Economists meet the challenge of unlimited wants with limited resources through finding the best way to allocate scarce resources.

- Economists balance marginal rather than average or total results and efforts. This often takes the form of maximizing profits or minimizing costs in decision-making.

- Economists emphasize the importance of incentives.

- Modern economists understand that the market mechanism does not solve all economic problems.

- Economists generally agree that free trade offers the possibility of gains for all participants.

- Economists consider externalities.

- Economists find competition and choice very significant for a viable operation of a modern economy.

- Economists frequently use mathematics to model economic questions. The assumptions that underlie these models drive debate among economists.

Notes

[1] This applies to one of the authors personally as well. In 1971, Michael Szenberg's dissertation, submitted by Victor R. Fuchs, won the Irving Fisher Award. Paul A. Samuelson was a member of the committee granting the prize. Other members of the committee included Maurice Allais (1988 Nobel Laureate), Kenneth Boulding, Milton Friedman (1976 Nobel Laureate), and Egon Neuberger. The study was subsequently published as *The Economics of the Israeli Diamond Industry*, with an Introduction by Milton Friedman. This opened new vistas for Szenberg, as Samuelson has continued to support his work.

[2] This volume is written to be accessible to a general audience. To delve into Samuelson's contributions from a critical perspective, please see our forthcoming companion volume, *Samuelsonian Economics and the 21st Century.*

[3] Personal correspondence, 2004.

[4] *Maariv*, "Literary Supplement," weekend edition in the 1990s. Interestingly, when Proust first wrote his monumental seven-volume tome, *Remembrance of Things Past*, no one would publish it. In fact, he had to use his own funds to publish the first volume. Yet, this experience did nothing to fill Proust's heart with empathy for young writers or to enhance his reverence for the human spirit.

[5] Hull 1988, 32.

[6] Gilbert 1991, 887.

[7] Hentoff 2004, XIX.

[8] For example, his recent article, "Why Ricardo and Mill Rebut and Confirm Arguments of Mainstream Economists Supporting Globalization," published in the *Journal of Economic Perspectives*, Summer 2004, created a stir and received coverage by the international press.

[9] Arrow 1995, 44.

[10] Stiglitz 2001; Samuelson 2003, 1.

[11] History buffs will note that the Secretary of the Interior at the time, Franklin K. Lane, directly linked the U.S. entry into WWI to the *Lusitania* attacks. Said Lane, "We are fighting Germany because she sought to terrorize us and then to fool us. We could not believe that Germany would do what she said she would do upon the seas. Yet, we still hear the piteous cries of children coming out, out of the sea where the *Lusitania* went down, and Germany has never asked forgiveness of the world." The Library of Congress provides a recording of this

speech online at memory.loc.gov/learn/collections/nforum/sound/lane. ra. For us, this event evokes the atrocities committed on September 11, 2001, approximately three blocks from the academic institution of two of the authors, which is located in Lower Manhattan.

[12]Silk 1976, 4.

[13]Clarence Darrow, of course, was a prominent leftist, known for his work as a labor and criminal lawyer. For more about Darrow, see the Clarence Darrow home page at www.law.umkc.edu/faculty/projects/ftrials/DARROW.HTM.

[14]Silk 1976, 7. Samuelson also tells of how Shoesmith left $2 million to the University of Chicago upon her death.

[15]*Ibid.*

[16]Samuelson 1972a, 9.

[17]Samuelson and Nordhaus 1995, xxix. Director's course was a remedial class that Samuelson had to take because he entered the University of Chicago one quarter late.

[18]*Ibid.*

[19]Bronfenbrenner 2004, 97. Bronfenbrenner also describes Viner as "meticulously fair," and notes "Viner expressed . . . regrets at having discouraged students by the harshness of his grading and classroom manner." Viner was also a matchmaker of sorts, albeit inadvertently. Milton Friedman tells of how he met his wife, in Viner's class: "it so happened that a fellow classmate was a beautiful young lady by the name of Rose Director (Aaron Director's sister). Because Viner seated people alphabetically, she sat next to me, and that too has shaped my whole life. We were married some years later. . . . (Friedman 1995, 85)."

[20]Samuelson 1972a, 8.

[21]In the essay in Chapter 5, Lawrence Klein remarks that at some point Samuelson's nature became softer. This is remarkable. There is a Mishnaic story in *Kidushin* by Tiferet Israel that Moses had negative traits such as rashness. But as Moses tells an inquiring king, had he not fought against his nature to become a good person he would be no better than a piece of dry wood. Thus, it was Moses' ability to overcome his nature that brought him the leadership of the Israelites. Indeed, modern psychology tells us how difficult it is to change one's nature, and succeed in improving oneself.

[22]Bronfenbrenner 2004, 97.

[23]*Ibid.*

[24]Personal correspondence, 2004.

[25]Samuelson 1998, 1376.

[26]Samuelson n.d., 4.

[27]Samuelson 1998, 1376.

[28]Samuelson n.d., 2.

[29]*Ibid.*, 6.

[30]Samuelson 1998, 1376. More about the interaction between Hansen and Samuelson in Chapter 2.

[31]*Ibid.* We will discuss Samuelson's views of economics as science or art in Chapter 3.

[32]Samuelson 1970a.

[33]Bergson 1992, 61. Upon Bergson's passing, Samuelson is quoted as saying: "Bergson would be on anyone's short list for a Nobel Prize." (*Harvard University Gazette*, May 1, 2003.)

[34]Tenner 1998.

[35]*Ibid.*

[36]Breit and Spencer 1995, 66.

[37]Samuelson 1998, 1376.

[38]Breit and Spencer 1995, 73.

[39]Samuelson 1998, 1376.

[40]Samuelson's daughter Jane teaches at Kings College at the University of London. Five other children live in the Boston area, and his oldest son, William, is a professor at Boston University teaching Managerial Economics. Samuelson also has fifteen grandchildren. Samuelson is currently married to Risha Samuelson, a painter. Alan Brown tells us of the following anecdote, attributed to Samuelson. Samuelson was asked how many children he had. His response, according to legend: "First we got one, then we got two, then we got three, then we got scared."

[41]Samuelson 1947. The original version also carried the subtitle *The Operational Significance of Economic Theory*.

[42]Lo 2001, 8.

[43]Samuelson and Nordhaus 1992, xxv.

[44]Personal correspondence, 2004.

[45]Breit and Ransom 1998, 110.

[46]Samuelson 1998, 1378. It brings to mind today's technology of digital printing in which no copyright will be returned to the author and no book will go out of print because in digital printing there is no advantage to economies of scale.

[47]*Ibid.*

[48]Samuelson 1983, 897. Samuelson's experience with Burbank differs from that of James Tobin, who writes positively about Burbank. (See Tobin, 1981; also see Galbraith, 1981).

[49]Samuelson 1998, 1377.

[50]Samuelson 1983, 89.

[51]Interestingly, the two schools strongly considered merging twice, 1897 and 1914, but faculty and alumni resistance prevented the union.

[52]Sobel 1980, 101. It is particularly ironic that Samuelson's nephew, Lawrence H. Summers, a prominent economist on his own, is currently the twenty-seventh President of Harvard University. A study by John Golden and Fred Carstensen found that while the total publication output of the economics department at MIT was not among the top economics department outputs between 1901–1940, from 1941–1989 MIT was among the top four (the study only extends until 1989) (Golden and Carstensen 1995, 73–77).

[53]Stiglitz 2001.

[54]Merton 1987.

[55]Personal correspondence, 2004.

[56]Personal correspondence, 2004.

[57]Personal correspondence, 2004.

[58]Samuelson and Nordhaus 1995, xxv.

[59]Silk 1976, 18.

[60]Private conversation, 2004.

[61]Samuelson 1962, 1–18.

[62]Samuelson 1992, 247.

[63]*Ibid.*

[64]Personal correspondence, 2004.

[65]Personal correspondence, 2004.

[66]Personal correspondence, 2004.

[67]Personal correspondence, 2004.

[68]Personal correspondence, 2004.

[69]Breit and Spencer 1995, 22–23.

[70]Personal correspondence, 2004.

[71]Indeed, the ability to come up with "wild" turns of phrase is to be expected from a *Newsweek* columnist. Two longer personal recollections of Samuelson as a teacher, from Avinash Dixit and Lawrence R. Klein, are included in Chapter 5.

[72]See *The Collected Scientific Papers of Paul A. Samuelson*, various years.

[73]Samuelson 1992, 236; Samuelson 1970a.

[74]Samuelson 1992, 236.

[75]Similarly, Arthur Okun urges us to "put some rationality into equality and some humanity into efficiency" (Okun 1975, 120).

[76]Samuelson 1992, 238. We discuss the relation between science and economics in Chapter 3.

[77] *Ibid.*

[78] Samuelson 1970a.

[79] Tosefta: *Baba Kamma*, 2.12. For example, consider his recent article, "Why Ricardo and Mill Rebut and Confirm Arguments of Mainstream Economists Supporting Globalization" published in the *Journal of Economic Perspectives*, Summer 2004, in which he argues that outsourcing offers not only opportunities and benefits but also risks and costs.

[80] Samuelson's experience of the "right" branding him as an enemy might have driven him to the left. His reaction is surprising, but rational.

[81] Silk 1976, 20.

[82] Samuelson 1992, 239.

[83] Private conversation, 2004.

[84] Samuelson 1992, 240.

[85] Personal correspondence 1992; Samuelson continues, "Arrow's Impossibility Theorem, in this view, applies to and cannot be escaped by the Buchanan-Hayek view of sacred property in the Smithian *status quo*. A rule of unanimity would freeze Stalin's totalitarianism into perpetuity, and thus represents Humpty-Dumptyism in its attempt to legitimize an historically extinct Whig *laissez faire.*"

[86] These include the *Global Competitiveness Report 2004–2005*, published by the World Economic Forum (www.weforum.org/site/homepublic. nsf/Content/Global+Competitiveness+Programme%5CGlobal+ Competitiveness+Report), and the *World Competitiveness Yearbook* published by the Institute of Management Development in Lausanne (www02.imd.ch/wcc).

[87] Personal correspondence, 2004.

[88] Note that it is important to distinguish between the *history of economic thought* that we define here and *economic history,* which is the narrative of economic activity over the ages.

[89] As the American history of slavery or the role of women in both Europe and the U.S. sadly tell us, not all individuals were granted these rights at that time.

[90] Many see symbolic importance in that the year of the book's publication was the year of the American independence.

[91] Samuelson 1969b, 1–11.

[92] Milton Friedman and other historians of the profession state that it was a tremendous failure of the Federal Reserve, which reduced the quantity of money rather than increasing it.

[93] Samuelson 1983, 6.

[94] Samuelson 1992, 245.

[95] Solow 1987.

[96]Personal correspondence, 2004.

[97]Stolper and Samuelson 1941, 58–73.

[98]Samuelson 1938, 61–71; Samuelson 1948a, 243–253.

[99]Samuelson 1960, 368.

[100]Personal correspondence, 2004. Kotlikof also recalls the time Samuelson referred "to Franco Modigliani at a meeting that I and Franco attended as MIT's most brilliant economist. Franco was very pleased—indeed, he was beaming as only Franco could beam."

[101]Bronfenbrenner 1982, 347.

[102]Samuelson 1939, 75–78. Samuelson directly attributes the accelerator to Hansen, writing: "Professor Hansen has developed a new model sequence. . . ."

[103]Samuelson 1959, 183.

[104]*Ibid.*

[105]Samuelson 1997, 155.

[106]Hicks 1937, 147–159.

[107]Samuelson 2004, xiii.

[108]Samuelson and Nordhaus 1995, 604.

[109]Paul Volcker was appointed as chairman of the Board of Governors by President Jimmy Carter in 1979. The main problem of the 1970s was, in Samuelson's word, "Stagflation". Inflation reached its double-digit peak during the Carter administration, when the FED continued to focus on the control of monetary targets. But from October 1979 to October 1982, the federal fund rate (the rate that banks charge other banks for overnight loans of their reserves with the FED) became increasingly volatile. Chairman Volcker then switched his targeting policy to the control of non-borrowed reserves. This policy did not have a fair chance then because deregulation, recessions in 1980 and 1981–1982, and financial innovations introduced uncertainty into the financial markets, creating an unstable demand for money. Eventually, in October 1982, the FED had to fall back on a policy to stabilize the federal fund rate.

[110]Samuelson and Nordhaus 1995, 610.

[111]Friedman 1953, 8–9.

[112]*Ibid.*, 15.

[113]Samuelson 1963, 232.

[114]*Ibid.*, 233.

[115]*Ibid.*, 236.

[116]Breit and Spencer 1995, 74.

[117]Private conversation, 2004.

[118]Samuelson 1992, 237–238.

[119]Samuelson 1976, 89.

[120]Friedman and Friedman 1998, 357 and footnote at the bottom of that page.

[121]Personal correspondence, 2004.

[122]Lindbeck 1970.

[123]Samuelson 1952, 56.

[124]For the curious, please note that the equation we use as an example is equation 15 from Samuelson's "Using Full Duality to Show that Simultaneously Additive Direct and Indirect Utilities Implies Unitary Price Elasticity of Demand." *Econometrica* 33, no. 4 (1965).

[125]In reality, economists often fail to show how "*a* leads to *b*," instead assuming that the reader can make the leap, using statements such as "obviously, *a* leads to *b*." This tends to happen because editors of journals don't have room to show all proofs, and assume that the reader will be sufficiently well-versed in mathematics to understand the relation.

[126]Of course, math can cause the reader to assume that the idea being described is more precise than it actually is. We will discuss criticism of the use of mathematics shortly.

[127]There are some techniques that are used by economists to present additional dimensions as well. For example, in an Edgeworth Box there can be six variables—although, as Alan Brown teases, "you have to stand on your head to get a good look at three of the six variables" (Personal correspondence, 2004).

[128]Samuelson 1972b, 257.

[129]Dorfman 1954, 374.

[130]Samuelson 1947, 6.

[131]Blinder 1999, 1.

[132]Samuelson 1954, 387–389.

[133]Lindbeck 2001.

[134]Hahn 1992, 163.

[135]David Novick 1954, 358.

[136]*Ibid.*

[137]Indeed, volume 36, number 4 of the *Review of Economics and Statistics* should not be missed by anyone seriously pondering the role of mathematics in economics.

[138]Samuelson 1954b, 381.

[139]*Ibid.*

[140]Samuelson 1952, 63–64.

[141]Samuelson 1952, 64.

[142] Blinder 1999, 4.

[143] See Ballard and Johnson 2004, 3–23; Durden and Ellis 1995, 343–346; and Anderson, Benjamin, and Fuss 1994, 99–119.

[144] For example, see Cohn, et al. 1998, 18–22.

[145] Samuelson 1952, 64–65.

[146] Hawking 1988, 9.

[147] Blinder 1999, 2.

[148] Hahn 1992, 163.

[149] Breit and Spencer 1995, 90–91.

[150] Samuelson 1992, 241.

[151] *Ibid.*, 244.

[152] Personal correspondence, 2004.

[153] Samuelson 1992, 240.

[154] Breit and Ransom 1998, 117.

[155] Samuelson 1992, 243.

[156] See Samuelson. "Unemployment Ahead." *New Republic* (September 11 and 18, 1944).

[157] Breit and Spencer 1995, 64.

[158] In 1981, 364 economists signed a letter to Margaret Thatcher warning her that her economic policies would lead to economic upheavals in the United Kingdom. We know now that the results were just the opposite. The economic boom started for the U. K. at this time.

[159] Samuelson 1992, 244.

[160] *Ibid.*, 243. For another type of eclecticism in economics, see Ray C. Fair's *Predicting Presidential Elections and Other Things*, where otherwise tedious methodologies are used to elucidate interesting topics, such as relationships, infidelity, and sports.

[161] Kornai 1990.

[162] Personal correspondence 2004.

[163] Peter Diamond of MIT tells us "Years ago, many members of the department faculty would go together to Red Sox games. Paul came along one time. During the game, he read a thermodynamics text, with notes being made in the margin (perhaps something about not being enough space to show his proof), while watching the game, and actually watching (Personal correspondence, 2004)."

[164] It is not only Samuelson's writing that is well tuned. Laurence J. Kotlikoff of Boston University recalls a recent speech that Samuelson gave at Boston University. "I had him give a talk to BU students last year and five hundred students showed up. He was amazing. He spoke for an hour and, as is his way, engaged in digressions within digressions to the point that I was wondering when and if he'd get back to the

main point. But sure enough, he brought everything back to square one in the last five minutes, tying each and every one of the links and loops together (Personal correspondence, 2004)."

[165] Personal correspondence, 2004. Alan Brown also describes how his wife, Barbara Brown, met Samuelson at a party. "When she was introduced, she asked: 'are you *the* Paul Samuelson?' To this, Samuelson politely replied, "and are you *the* Mrs. Barbara Brown?' This made Bobby heartily laugh, resolving the usual tension that surrounds new graduate students and their spouses as they meet distinguished faculty."

[166] Samuelson 1997, 154.

[167] *Ibid.*

[168] *Ibid.*

[169] Samuelson 1999, 353.

[170] McGraw, Jr. 1999, 355. Harold W. McGraw was then chairman emeritus of McGraw-Hill. December 8, 1941, of course, was one day after the Pearl Harbor attacks.

[171] Samuelson 1999, 354.

[172] Skousen 1997a.

[173] Excerpts from the newest edition as of this time can be viewed at www.mhhe.com/economics/samuelson.

[174] Nordhaus 1999, 358.

[175] *Ibid.*, 354.

[176] *Ibid.*, 354.

[177] Helpman 1998, 133.

[178] Personal Correspondence, 2004.

[179] For one academic's reflection on how *Economics* influenced his life, see Brady 2002.

[180] Samuelson 1997, 159.

[181] *Ibid.*

[182] Samuelson's fame has grown to the point where even his personality has been placed under the academic microscope. See Price 2002.

[183] Samuelson 1999, 354.

[184] Samuelson and Nordhaus 1995, xxix.

[185] Linder 1977, 5.

[186] Skousen 1997a, 147.

[187] *Ibid.*

[188] *Ibid.*, 139–140.

[189] Skousen 1997b, 198.

[190] Samuelson and Nordhaus 1989, 837.

[191] Skousen 1997b, 198.

[192] Samuelson 1999, 353.

[193] *Ibid.*

[194] Samuelson 1997, 155.

[195] *Ibid.*, 159.

[196] Private conversation, 2004.

[197] Garver and Hansen 1938; Kiekhoffer 1936; Slichter 1931; Fairchild, Furniss, and Buck 1936.

[198] Samuelson 1997, 154. Say's Law is discussed in Chapter 2 of our book.

[199] Solow 1999, 361.

[200] Fischer 1999, 363.

[201] Breit and Spencer 1995, 67.

[202] *Ibid.*

[203] *Ibid.*

[204] Lindbeck 2001.

[205] *Ibid.*

[206] Breit and Spencer 1995, 75.

[207] *Ibid.*, 74.

[208] Personal correspondence, 2004.

[209] Breit and Spencer 1995, 73.

[210] Private conversation, 2004.

[211] Samuelson 1999, 355.

[212] These sayings bring out a lifetime of intuition and learning from an outstanding scholar. The references included in the parentheses refer to the volume and page number of his five volumes of *Collected Scientific Papers*.

References

Anderson, G., Benjamin, D., and M. Fuss. "The Determinants of Success in University Introductory Economics Courses." *Journal of Economic Education* 25 (1994): 99–119.

Arrow, Kenneth. In *Lives of the Laureates: Thirteen Nobel Economists*, edited by W. Breit and R.W. Spencer. Cambridge, MA: MIT Press, 1995.

Ballard, C. L., and M. F. Johnson. "Basic Math Skills and Performance in an Introductory Economics Class." *Journal of Economic Education* 35, no. 1 (2004): 3–23.

Bartlett, R. L. "Attracting 'Otherwise Bright Students' to Economics 101." *American Economic Review* 85, no. 2 (1995): 362–366.

Bergson, Abram. "Recollections and Reflections of a Comparativist." In *Eminent Economists*, edited by Michael Szenberg. New York and London: Cambridge University Press, 1992.

Blinder, Alan S. "Economics Becomes a Science—or Does it?" *Millennium Symposium Papers*, American Philosophical Society, 1999. (Available at www.aps-pub.com/millennium/blinder.pdf)

Brady, Michael Emmett. "The Role of Samuelson's *Economics* in the Production of a Keynesian Economist." In *Paul Samuelson and the Foundations of Modern Economics*, edited by K. Puttaswamaiah. New Brunswick, NJ: Transaction Publishers, 2002.

Breit, William, and Roger L. Ransom. *Academic Scribblers*. 3rd ed. Princeton, NJ: Princeton University Press, 1998.

Breit, William and R. W. Spencer, eds. *Lives of the Laureates: Thirteen Nobel Economists*. 3rd ed. Cambridge, MA: MIT Press, 1995.

Bronfenbrenner, Martin. "On the Superlative in Samuelson," In *Samuelson and Neoclassical Economics*, edited by George F. Feiwel. Boston, MA: Kluwer-Nijhoff, 1982.

Bronfenbrenner, Martin. "Instead of a Philosophy of Life," In *Reflections of Eminent Economists*, edited by Michael Szenberg and Lall Ramrattan. Northampton, MA: Elgar, 2004.

Burtt, Jr., Everett J. *Social Perspectives in the History of Economic Theory.* New York: St. Martin's Press, 1972.

Canterbery, E. Ray. *The Making of Economics.* Belmont, CA: Wadsworth Publishing Company, 1980.

Chiang, Alpha C. *Fundamental Methods of Mathematical Economics.* New York: McGraw-Hill, 1984.

Cohn, E., Cohn, S., Hult, Jr., R. E., Balch, D. C., and J. Bradley, Jr. "The Effects of Mathematics Background on Student Learning in Principles of Economics." *Journal of Education for Business* 74, no. 1 (1998): 18–22.

Dorfman, Robert. "A Catechism: Mathematics in Social Science." *Review of Economics and Statistics* 36 (1954).

Durden, G., and L. Ellis. "The Effects of Attendance on Student Learning in Principles of Economics." *American Economic Review* 85 (1995): 343–346.

Fair, Ray C. *Predicting Presidential Elections and Other Things.* Palo Alto, CA: Stanford University Press, 2002.

Fairchild, Fred R., Furniss, Edgar S., and Norman S. Buck. *Elementary Economics.* New York: MacMillan, 1936.

Feiwel, George F. *Samuelson and Neoclassical Economics.* Boston: Kluwer-Nijhoff, 1982.

Fischer, Stanley. In "Samuelson's *Economics* at Fifty: Remarks on the Occasion of the Anniversary of Publication." *Journal of Economic Education* (Fall 1999).

Friedman, Milton. "The Methodology of Positive Economics," In *Essays in Positive Economics.* Chicago: University of Chicago Press, 1953.

Friedman, Milton, ed. *Studies in the Quantity Theory of Money.* Chicago: University of Chicago Press, 1956.

Friedman, Milton, and Rose D. Friedman. *Two Lucky People: Memoirs.* Chicago: University of Chicago Press, 1998.

Galbraith, J. K. *A Life in our Times.* Boston: Houghton Mifflin, 1981.

Garver, Fredric B., and Alvin Hansen. *Principles of Economics.* Boston: Ginn, 1938.

Gilbert, Martin. *Churchill, A Life.* New York: Henry Holt, 1991.

Golden, John and Fred Carstensen. "Twentieth Century Publications Performance in Five Leading Economics Journals, A Comment." *The American Economist* 39 (Fall 1995): 73–77.

Hahn, Frank "Autobiographical Notes with Reflections." In *Eminent Economists,* edited by Michael Szenberg. New York and London: Cambridge University Press, 1992.

Hahn, Frank. "Samuelson: A Personal Recollection," In *Paul Samuelson and the Foundations of Modern Economics,* edited by K. Puttaswamaiah. New Brunswick, NJ: Transaction Publishers, 2002.

Haney, Lewis H. *History of Economic Thought.* New York: Macmillan, 1949.

Hansen, Alvin H. *A Guide to Keynes.* New York: McGraw-Hill, 1953.

Hawking, Stephen. *A Brief History of Time.* New York: Bantam Books, 1988.

Helpman, Elhanan. "Doing Research." In *Passion and Craft,* edited by Michael Szenberg. Ann Arbor, MI: University of Michigan Press, 1998.

Hicks, John R. "Mr. Keynes and the Classics, A Suggested Reinterpretation." *Econometrica* 5 (1937): 147–159.

Hull, David. *An Evolutionary Account of the Social and Conceptual Development of Science.* Chicago: University of Chicago Press, 1988.

Hentoff, Nat. *American Music Is.* New York: Da Capo Press, 2004.

Kiekhoffer,William H. *Economic Principles, Problems and Policies.* New York: Appleton-Century, 1936.

Klein, Lawrence R. In *Lives of the Laureates: Thirteen Nobel Economists.* 3rd ed., edited by W. Breit and R. W. Spencer. Cambridge, MA: MIT Press, 1995.

Kornai, János. *The Road to a Free Economy: Shifting from a Socialist System.* New York: W.W. Norton, 1990.

Lindbeck, Assar. Presentation Speech. Nobel Foundation (1970). (Available at www.nobel.se/economics/laureates/1970/press.html)

Lindbeck, Assar. "The Sveriges Riksbank (Bank of Sweden) Prize in Economic Sciences in Memory of Alfred Nobel 1969–2000." In *The Nobel Prize: The First 100 Years*, edited by Agneta Wallin Levinovitz and Nils Ringertz. London: Imperial College Press / London: World Scientific Publishing Co. Ltd., 2001. (Available at www.nobel.se/economics/articles/lindbeck)

Linder, Marc, in collaboration with Julius Sensat. *Anti-Samuelson*. New York: Urizen Books, 1977.

Lo, Andrew. "Bubble, Rubble, Finance in Trouble." Working Paper (2001). (Available at http://www.alphasimplex.com/Papers/paper3.pdf)

McCloskey, D. N. "Other Things Equal: Samuelsonian Economics." *Eastern Economic Journal* 28, no. 3 (2002): 425–430.

McGraw, Jr., Harold W. Contribution to "Samuelson's *Economics* at Fifty: Remarks on the Occasion of the Anniversary of Publication." *Journal of Economic Education* (Fall 1999).

Merton, Robert C. "Robert C. Merton—Autobiography." Nobel Foundation (1987). (Available at www.nobel.se/economics/laureates/1997/merton-autobio.html)

Nordhaus, William D. Contribution to "Samuelson's *Economics* at Fifty: Remarks on the Occasion of the Anniversary of Publication." *Journal of Economic Education* (Fall 1999).

Novick, David. "Mathematics, Logic, Quantity, and Method." *Review of Economics and Statistics* 36 (1954).

Okun, Arthur M. *Equality and Efficiency.* Washington, D.C.: Brookings Institution, 1975.

Price, B. B. "Samuelson the Vain." In *Paul Samuelson and the Foundations of Modern Economics*, edited by K. Puttaswamaiah. New Brunswick, NJ: Transaction Publishers, 2002.

Puttaswamaiah, K. "Contributions of Paul Samuelson." In *Paul Samuelson and the Foundations of Modern Economics*, edited by K. Puttaswamaiah. New Brunswick, NJ: Transaction Publishers, 2002.

Samuelson, Paul A. "Our Wassily: W.W. Leontief (1905–1999)." (n.d.). (Available at policy.rutgers.edu/cupr/iioa/SamuelsonOurWassily.pdf)

Samuelson, Paul A. "A Note on the Pure Theory of Consumer's Behavior." *Economica* 5 (1938): 61–71.

Samuelson, Paul A. "Interactions between the Multiplier Analysis and the Principle of Acceleration." *Review of Economics and Statistics* (May 1939): 75–78.

Samuelson, Paul A. "Unemployment Ahead." *New Republic* (September 11 and 18, 1944).

Samuelson, Paul A. *Foundations of Economic Analysis.* Harvard Economic Studies vol. 80 (1947).

Samuelson, Paul A. "Consumption Theory in Terms of Revealed Preference." *Economica* (1948a): 243–253.

Samuelson, Paul A. "International Trade and the Equalisation of Factor Prices." *Economic Journal* 58 (1948b): 163–84.

Samuelson, Paul A. "International Factor-Price Equalisation Once Again." *Economic Journal* 59 (1949): 181–197.

Samuelson, Paul A. "Economic Theory and Mathematics — an Appraisal." *American Economic Review* 42 (1952).

Samuelson, Paul A. "Price of Factors and Goods in General Equilibrium." *Review of Economic Studies* (1953): 1–20.

Samuelson, Paul A. "The Pure Theory of Public Expenditure." *Review of Economics and Statistics* 36 (1954a): 387–89.

Samuelson, Paul A. "Some Psychological Aspects of Mathematics and Economics." *Review of Economics and Statistics* 36 (1954b): 380–386.

Samuelson, Paul A. "Diagrammatic Exposition of a Theory of Public Expenditure." *Review of Economics and Statistics* 37 (1955): 350–56.

Samuelson, Paul A. "Aspects of Public Expenditure Theories." *Review of Economics and Statistics* 40 (1958): 332–38.

Samuelson, Paul A. "Alvin Hansen and the Interactions between the Multiplier Analysis and the Principle of Acceleration." *Review of Economics and Statistics* (May 1959).

Samuelson, Paul A. "An Extension of the Le Chatelier Principle." *Econometrica* 28, no. 2 (April 1960): 368.

Samuelson, Paul A. "Economists and the History of Ideas." *American Economic Review* 52, no. 1 (March 1962): 1–18.

Samuelson, Paul A. "Problems of Methodology—Discussion." *American Economic Review* 53 (May 1963).

Samuelson, Paul A. "Proof that Properly Anticipated Prices Fluctuate Randomly." *Industrial Management Review* 6 (1965a): 41–49.

Samuelson, Paul A. "Rational Theory of Warrant Pricing." *Industrial Management Review* 6 (1965b): 13–39.

Samuelson, Paul A. "Using Full Duality to Show that Simultaneously Additive Direct and Indirect Utilities Implies Unitary Price Elasticity of Demand." *Econometrica* 33, no. 4 (1965c): 781–796.

Samuelson, Paul A. "General Proof that Diversification Pays." *Journal of Financial and Quantitative Analysis* 2 (1967): 1–13.

Samuelson, Paul A. "Lifetime Portfolio Selection by Dynamic Stochastic Programming." *Review of Economics and Statistics* 51 (1969): 239–246.

Samuelson, Paul A. "The Way of an Economist." In *International Economic Relations: Proceedings of the Third Congress of the International Economic Association*, edited by Paul A. Samuelson. London: Macmillan, 1969: 1–11.

Samuelson, Paul A. "How I Became an Economist." Nobel Foundation (1970a). (Available at www.nobel.se/economics/articles/samuelson-2)

Samuelson, Paul A. "The Fundamental Approximation Theorem of Portfolio Analysis in Terms of Means, Variances, and Higher Moments." *Review of Economic Studies* 37 (1970b): 537–42.

Samuelson, Paul A. "Jacob Viner 1892–1970." *Journal of Political Economy* 80, no. 1 (1972a).

Samuelson, Paul A. "Maximum Principles in Analytical Economics." *American Economic Review* 62, no. 3 (1972b): 249–262.

Samuelson, Paul A. "Milton Friedman." *Newsweek* (October 25, 1976): 89.

Samuelson, Paul A. "Economics in a Golden Age: A Personal Memoir." In *Paul Samuelson and Modern Economic Theory*, edited by C.E. Brown and R.M. Solow. New York: McGraw-Hill, 1983.

Samuelson, Paul A. *The Collected Scientific Papers of Paul A. Samuelson*, edited by Joseph E. Stiglitz. Vols. 1 and 2. Cambridge, MA: MIT Press, 1966.

Samuelson, Paul A. *The Collected Scientific Papers of Paul A. Samuelson*, edited by Robert C. Merton. Vol. 3. Cambridge, MA: MIT Press, 1972.

Samuelson, Paul A. *The Collected Scientific Papers of Paul A. Samuelson*, edited by H. Nagatani and K. Crowley. Vol. 4. Cambridge, MA: MIT Press, 1978.

Samuelson, Paul A. *The Collected Scientific Papers of Paul A. Samuelson*, edited by Kate Crowley. Vol. 5. Cambridge, MA: MIT Press, 1986.

Samuelson, Paul A., and William D. Nordhaus. *Economics*. 13th ed. New York: McGraw Hill, 1989.

Samuelson, Paul A. "My Life Philosophy: Policy Credos and Working Ways" in *Eminent Economists*, edited by Michael Szenberg. New York and London: Cambridge University Press, 1992.

Samuelson, Paul A., and William D. Nordhaus. *Economics*. 15th ed. New York: McGraw Hill, 1995.

Samuelson, Paul A. "Credo of a Lucky Textbook Author." *Journal of Economic Perspectives* (Spring 1997).

Samuelson, Paul A. "How Foundations Came to Be." *Journal of Economic Literature* 36, no. 3 (1998).

Samuelson, Paul A. Contribution to "Samuelson's *Economics* at Fifty: Remarks on the Occasion of the Anniversary of Publication." *Journal of Economic Education* (Fall 1999).

Samuelson, Paul A. "Portrait of the Master as an MIT Graduate Student." Presentation for *Economics for an Imperfect World: A Conference for Joe Stiglitz's 60th Birthday.* 2003.

Samuelson, Paul A. "Foreword." In *New Frontiers in Economics*, edited by Michael Szenberg and Lall Ramrattan. New York and London: Cambridge University Press, 2004.

Samuelson, Paul A. "Why Ricardo and Mill Rebut and Confirm Arguments of Mainstream Economists Supporting Globalization." *Journal of Economic Perspectives* (Summer 2004).

Silk, Leonard. *The Economists.* New York: Basic Books, 1976.

Skousen, Mark. "The Perseverance of Paul Samuelson's Economics." *Journal of Economic Perspectives* (Spring, 1997a): 137–152.

Skousen, Mark. "Welcome Back, Professor." *Forbes Magazine* (September 22, 1997b): 198.

Slichter, Sumner H. *Modern Economic Society.* New York: Henry Holt, 1931.

Sobel, Robert. *The Worldly Economists.* New York: The Free Press, 1980.

Solow, Robert M. "Robert M. Solow—Autobiography." Nobel Foundation (1987). (Available at www.nobel.se/economics/laureates/1987/solow-autobio.html).

Solow, Robert M. Contribution to "Samuelson's *Economics* at Fifty: Remarks on the Occasion of the Anniversary of Publication." *Journal of Economic Education* (Fall 1999).

Stiglitz, Joseph. "Joseph E. Stiglitz—Autobiography." Nobel Foundation (2001). (Available at www.nobel.se/economics/laureates/2001/stiglitz-autobio.html).

Stolper, Wolfgang, and Paul A. Samuelson. "Protection and Real Wages." *Review of Economic Studies* 9 (1941): 58–73.

Szenberg, Michael. *The Economics of the Israeli Diamond Industry*, with an Introduction by Milton Friedman. New York: Basic Books, 1973.

Szenberg, Michael, ed. *Passion and Craft*, with a Foreword by Paul A. Samuelson. Ann Arbor, MI: University of Michigan Press, 1998.

Szenberg, Michael, ed. *Eminent Economists, Their Life Philosophies.* New York and London: Cambridge University Press, 1992.

Szenberg, Michael, and Lall Ramrattan, eds. *New Frontiers in Economics,* with a Foreword by Paul A. Samuelson. New York and London: Cambridge University Press, 2004a.

Szenberg, Michael, and Lall Ramrattan, eds. *Reflections of Eminent Economists,* with a Foreword by Kenneth Arrow. Northampton, MA: Elgar, 2004b.

E. Tenner. "Environment for Genius?" *Harvard Magazine* (November-December 1998).

Tobin, James. "James Tobin—Autobiography." Nobel Foundation (1981). (Available at www.nobel.se/economics/laureates/1981/tobin-autobio.html).

About the Authors

Michael Szenberg, Ph.D. is a Distinguished Professor of Economics and the Chair of the Finance and Economics Department at the Lubin School of Business, Pace University. He has a Ph.D. in Economics from the City University of New York (1970), a B.A. in Economics (summa cum laude) from Long Island University (1963), and a Diploma from the Air Force Aeronautics School. Szenberg is a recipient of the Kenan Award for excellence in teaching, and received Pace University's Award for Distinguished Faculty Service. Szenberg also serves as editor-in-chief of the *American Economist* and as consultant to private and governmental agencies.

He has authored and edited several award-winning books, which have been translated into several languages. His *Economics of the Israeli Diamond Industry*, with an Introduction by Milton Friedman, won the Irving Fisher Monograph Award. The last two books, *New Frontiers in Economics*, with a Foreword by Paul A. Samuelson, was published in 2004 by Cambridge University Press and *Reflections of Eminent Economists*, with a Foreword by Kenneth Arrow, was published in 2004 by Elgar Publishing Co. The two volumes were co-edited with Lall Ramrattan. You can visit Dr. Szenberg's web page at webpage.pace.edu/mszenberg.

Aron A. Gottesman, Ph.D. is an Assistant Professor in the Department of Finance and Economics at the Lubin School of Business at Pace University. He has a Ph.D. in Finance (2001), an M.B.A. in Finance (1997), and a B.A. in Psychology (1994), all from York University in Toronto.

Professor Gottesman has taught graduate and undergraduate courses on investment analysis, derivative securities, and the theory of capital markets, and has presented corporate seminars on finance and risk-related topics. He has consulted to both private corporations and governments in the areas of portfolio analysis, insurance, and banking. He has received a number of awards, research grants, and scholarships, including a research grant and doctoral fellowship from the Canadian Social Sciences and Humanities Research Council (SSHRC). In 2001 he received an award for the best paper on financial institutions at the Northern Finance Association Meetings.

Professor Gottesman's research interests include financial markets, financial intermediation, corporate finance, and the history of economic thought. He has published a number of articles on finance and economics in academic and policy journals, including the *Journal of Banking and Finance*, the *Journal of Financial Markets*, and *The National Interest*, among others, and is an Associate Editor of the *American Economist*. Gottesman has also coauthored a book titled *Insurance Logic*, the second edition of which was published in 2005. You can visit Professor Gottesman's Web page at www.arongottesman.com.

Lall Ramrattan, Ph.D. received his Ph.D. from the New School University in 1986. He currently teaches Economics at the University of California, Berkeley Extension. He has published many articles in professional journals on a variety of topics. His books include *New Frontiers in Economics*, with a Foreword by Paul A. Samuelson, published in 2004 by Cambridge University Press and *Reflections of Eminent Economists*, with a Foreword by Kenneth Arrow, published in 2004 by Elgar Publishing Co. The two volumes were co-edited with Michael Szenberg. Currently, his interest is in the application of economic models to industry and country studies.

Vignette Contributors

Tony Atkinson is the Warden of Nuffield College, Oxford University.
Source: www.nuff.ox.ac.uk/economics/people/atkinson.htm

Jagdish Bhagwati is University Professor at Columbia University and
Senior Fellow at the Council on Foreign Relations.
Source: www.columbia.edu/~jb38

Alan A. Brown was professor of economics at the University of Windsor,
Ontario.

James Buchanan is the Advisory General Director at the Center for Study
of Public Choice, George Mason University. He won the 1986 Nobel
Memorial Prize in Economic Science.
Source: www.gmu.edu/jbc/faculty_bios/buchananvita.html

Peter Diamond is an Institute Professor at the Massachusetts Institute
of Technology.
Source: econ-www.mit.edu/faculty/download_cv.php?prof_id=pdiamond

Avinash Dixit is the John J. F. Sherrerd '52 University Professor of
Economics at Princeton University.
Source: www.princeton.edu/~dixitak/home

Milton Friedman is a Senior Research Fellow at the Hoover Institution,
Stanford, California. He was the recipient of the 1976 Nobel Memorial
Prize for economic science.
Source: www-hoover.stanford.edu/bios/friedman.html

Frank Hahn is a professor of economics at Cambridge University.
Source: cepa.newschool.edu/het/profiles/hahn.htm

Bengt Holmstrom is the Paul A. Samuelson Professor of Economics at
the Massachusetts Institute of Technology.
Source: econ-www.mit.edu/faculty/download_cv.php?prof_id=bengt

Lawrence Klein is the Benjamin Franklin Professor Emeritus of Economics
at the University of Pennsylvania. He won the 1980 Nobel Memorial
Prize in Economic Science.
Source: www.econ.upenn.edu/cgi-bin/mecon/bin/view.cgi?id=18

János Kornai is a Permanent Fellow at Collegium Budapest, Hungary and Emeritus Professor at Harvard University.
Source: post.economics.harvard.edu/faculty/kornai/kornai.html

Laurence J. Kotlikoff is a professor of economics at Boston University.
Source: econ.bu.edu/kotlikoff

Rachel McCulloch is the Rosen Family Professor of International Finance at the International Business School at Brandeis University.
Source: www.brandeis.edu/global/faculty_detail.php?faculty_id=26

Perry Mehrling is the Chair of the Department of Economics at Barnard College, Columbia University.
Source: cedar.barnard.columbia.edu/faculty/mehrling/mehrling.html

Robert C. Merton is the John and Natty McArthur University Professor at Harvard Business School. He won the 1997 Nobel Memorial Prize in Economic Science.
Source: dor.hbs.edu/fi_redirect.jhtml?facInfo=bio&facEmId=rmerton

James Poterba is the Mitsui Professor of Economics and the Associate Head of the Economics Department at the Massachusetts Institute of Technology.
Source: econ-www.mit.edu/faculty/index.htm?prof_id=poterba&type=shortbio

Kenneth Rogoff is the Thomas D. Cabot Professor of Public Policy and Professor of Economics at Harvard University.
Source: post.economics.harvard.edu/faculty/rogoff/rogoff.html

Thomas Schelling is a Distinguished University Professor at the University of Maryland School of Public Affairs.
Source: www.puaf.umd.edu/faculty/people/schellingm.html

Joseph Stiglitz is a University Professor at Columbia University. He won the 2001 Nobel Memorial Prize in Economic Science.
Source: www-1.gsb.columbia.edu/faculty/jstiglitz

Peter Temin is the Elisha Gray II Professor of Economics at the Massachusetts Institute of Technology.
Source: econ-www.mit.edu/faculty/?prof_id=ptemin

Richard Zeckhauser is the Frank Plumpton Ramsey Professor of Political Economy at Harvard University's John F. Kennedy School of Government.
Source: ksghome.harvard.edu/~.RZeckhauser.Acad

Index

Printed in the United States
97243LV00004B/58/A